Signs To Life

READING AND RESPONDING
TO JOHN'S GOSPEL

KENDRA HALOVIAK VALENTINE

Signs to Life

READING AND RESPONDING TO JOHN'S GOSPEL

KENDRA HALOVIAK VALENTINE

WITH CAROLYN RICKETT, DANIEL REYNAUD, JANE FERNANDEZ AND NATHAN BROWN

Printed and published by
SIGNS PUBLISHING COMPANY
Victoria, Australia

Proudly published and printed in Australia by
Signs Publishing Company
Warburton, Victoria.

This book was
Edited by Nathan Brown, Kerry Arbuckle and Lindy Schneider
Cover photograph by argus/shutterstock.com
Cover design by Ashlea Malycha
Typeset in Berkeley Book 11/14.5

ISBN (print edition) 978 1 921292 91 0
ISBN (ebook edition) 978 1 921292 92 7

To my parents,
Bert and Mary Haloviak,
whose love of Scripture inspired my own.

Contents

Introduction

Reading and Responding to John's Gospel

Students in my biblical studies classes and church members attending seminars often remind me of the Ethiopian eunuch we read about in Acts 8:26–40. They typically articulate deep convictions about Scripture, read it and have a passionate desire to study and understand it, but often do not know how or where to begin. The Ethiopian eunuch's story tells us that the apostle Philip was moved by the Holy Spirit to run up alongside the stranger's chariot. It was then that Philip heard that the Ethiopian was reading aloud from the prophet Isaiah. Philip asked with some apprehension: "Do you understand what you are reading?" But the man reading Scripture replied, "'How can I unless someone guides me?' And he invited Philip to get in and sit beside him" (Acts 8:30, 31).

This book is an invitation to "sit beside" others and learn new things as we read the Gospel of John together. Often its pages are not as "plain" as we first thought. And how do we actually do what we are so often told, that is, to "take the Bible just as it is"?[1] What does it mean to "take the Bible just as it is"? Reading biblical passages in English already moves a reader from the Bible's original languages to interpretations. And certainly whenever a reader says, "This is what the passage means to me . . ." she has left what is "literal" for what is meaningful. Isn't that inevitable (and a good thing)? Isn't that the only way the Bible comes alive for us? The contributors to this book believe that the gospel according to John (also referred to as John's gospel or the Fourth Gospel) should be read and re-read "just as it is"—as an inspired work but also as a work of art that should be taken seriously as a literary whole.

1

This present volume begins with several assumptions that are highlighted by its title: "Signs to Life: Reading and Responding to John's Gospel." First, the word "signs" refers to the seven miracles (called "signs") spoken about in the first half of John's gospel. Like signposts alongside the road or highway, the signs are not the destination, but they do guide readers there. Each sign points to Jesus, the focus of John's gospel. When characters in this gospel ask for more signs, they betray their own location—they have not yet arrived at the place where John wants them to be. But the author does not give up on such characters. He keeps trying to guide them—and his readers—toward Jesus.

The word "signs" also suggests that this particular Johannine story of Jesus' life does not leave readers alone to figure everything out. Instead, the author gives literary cues within the narrative that encourage readers to follow the "signs" along the way and to respond appropriately. These cues, for example, are found in such things as narrator's comments, character development, irony and repetition. Different readers will notice different parts of the story and will "fill in the gaps" in their own ways.[2] Readers who follow the signs and cues learn that this Jesus offers "life abundantly" (see John 10:10).

Readers from different social locations will imagine ways that Jesus gave life in the past and how the Spirit continues to give life in the present. John's gospel was preserved by its first readers and has been valued by readers in every generation since. Contemporary readers continue to read and respond to this good news. Each engagement inevitably (and thankfully) involves the presuppositions and insights each reader brings to the act of reading. As readers pay close attention to the literary cues, some readers' presuppositions will be challenged, opening up still more possibilities for insights and new understandings. Because of the richness of possible reader responses, the life offered in this gospel is certainly abundant.

Reading for my church

Part I of this book contains seven sermons reflecting on stories found in the first half of John's gospel. They represent a reading from a particular point of view—my point of view. I am a Seventh-day Adventist Christian who serves my church by teaching New Testament studies classes in the divinity school of one of its universities. After being asked by the president of my denomination to speak to the employees at the church's world headquarters for a week of worships in 2004, I prepared by reading John's gospel with that specific task in mind.[3] My interpretations on that occasion were shaped by a particular audience I knew quite well.

Since my parents gave most of their professional lives to serving at our church's world headquarters, I grew up walking its halls and hearing employees—both local employees and visiting international employees—discuss and debate various actions and visions for the world church. Some employees I have known all my life. Some employees have children who were my classmates through elementary school, high school and into college. Some employees had been my parishioners, and a few recently hired employees had been my students in college religion classes. In preparing the sermons for that week, this diverse community of church leaders kept joining me in my imagination as I read. Their issues, questions and convictions shaped my reading of John's gospel. As I prepared I was—in my mind and heart—in conversation with people I knew would be present during that week.

This would not be the first time I experienced a week of worships at the church's world headquarters. When my brother and I were in elementary school, we attended a week of morning devotional meetings for the employees. We really did not have a choice. It was necessary because our parents had agreed to provide the music for the week, and we were too young to stay home alone.

At the end of that long week, then-General Conference president, Neal Wilson, presented the two of us with a gift. He said it was for sitting so quietly on the front row all week! The gift was a book by writer Marye Trim, entitled *Tell Me About Sister White*.[4] It was a slim volume that introduced children to Ellen White, the most important founder of the Seventh-day Adventist Church. I remember the moment President Wilson handed me that book. It was a moment when I could tangibly feel and appreciate that my church community had special stories, traditions and ideas it valued, and it was passing these on to me.

I believe the Adventist Church has valuable insights and important ideas to pass on to others. Of course, our most cherished beliefs are those we share with Christians of all denominations. But there are other beliefs that are important and that distinguish this particular faith community. Later in graduate school, I was delighted to find people of various faith traditions eager to hear what my Adventism contributes to conversations about God, community, the life of faith, salvation and the future. It is important to ask what Adventist Christianity contributes to such conversations.

While considering ways the Fourth Gospel addresses current questions and issues within Adventism, these readings and responses are prepared with a desire to be inclusive of friends, neighbours or work colleagues who might not identify with the Adventist community. The gospel of John has spoken to people of various religious convictions for almost 2000 years—and continues to do so. So in a book such as this, we join "a great cloud of witnesses" that expands far beyond any one particular church family. When I use Seventh-day Adventist Church-speak, it is not meant to be exclusive but to allow for specificity, to be able to talk candidly about the faith tradition I know and love.

As readers, we all read and retell the Jesus story in light of our own concerns and questions, stories and experiences or in the light of the concerns of those to whom we are reading. We do this even as we "take the Bible as it is." The author of John's gospel was no different; he did the same thing. In his 2011 book *The Riddles of the Fourth Gospel*, Paul Anderson points out how John's gospel functions in a distinctive way as a "dialogical" text.[5] By this he means that the issues and questions that concerned John and his community of fellow believers shaped the particular way he told the story of Jesus. And that kind of shaping is inevitable.

Describing the Fourth Gospel as a "dialogical" text means that the author of the gospel is in conversation with others in his community— for John that means Jewish Christians, Gentile Christians and Jews. These conversations helped create the work just as they create the interpretations readers will give to the stories. As the signs, encounter stories and dialogues were being selected by the author and shaped in their telling, the issues, questions and convictions of those first-century believers were never far away.[6]

At the same time, in his careful and thoughtful crafting of the story of Jesus, inspired by the Spirit, this author did *not* have the questions and issues of our particular communities in his thoughts while composing the gospel. It was not like he leaped over all the centuries between his world and ours. But we bring to the reading of his story our 21st-century hopes and fears and questions. And the Spirit speaks to us today through the story.

Uniquely, the writer of the Fourth Gospel uses the language of "signs" to explore the life of Jesus and its implications for the present. This gospel contains seven signs—all placed in the first half of the book. Commentators often refer to this first part of the book as the "Book of Signs," some even wondering if such a book existed prior to the writing of the gospel as a whole. Most of the signs are miracles unique to this gospel.[7] When the signs finish, the narrative shifts to the death of Jesus. In this study, we will consider the signs in light of the Fourth Gospel's portrayal of the final events of Jesus' life.

The readings represented in the seven sermons are inevitably shaped by my journey as an Adventist who grew up "sitting beside" other Adventists as we read Scripture together. For example, I knew that the "signs" language comes with baggage for an Adventist community anxiously awaiting the "signs of the end" for almost 170 years.[8] John's scenes of abundant water bring to mind the Adventist commitment to adult baptism by immersion. Sabbath miracles remind many in my community of childhood checklists of proper Sabbath behaviour. John's scene of the Eucharist with Jesus talking about "eating his flesh" would not typically be chosen for Communion Sabbath in an Adventist church lest the uninformed visitor mistakenly think we were Catholic. Lazarus' bodily resurrection affirms the Adventist understanding—and fundamental belief—concerning the "state of the dead."

The seven sermons in this book illustrate the important hermeneutical principle that when we read a biblical text within the context of a faith community's current questions and convictions, we are being faithful to the way the text was originally created. And being aware of the fact that we read in this way, we are more likely to respond to the ways the text both affirms and challenges our convictions. The same Spirit who was at work in the gospel's creation remains with readers in every age.

Other readers and responses

Part II of the book contains the contributions of four other Adventist readers reflecting on their reading of—and their responses to—John's gospel in their here and now. In some cases, the reader responds to one of the seven signs narrated in the text. In other cases, the reader considers a passage or passages in the gospel not discussed earlier. This second section highlights the interdisciplinary nature of contemporary interpretations. Reading is enhanced by readers who bring new questions, presuppositions and insights to the texts.

All four of these readers are associated with Avondale College of Higher Education, located in Cooranbong, New South Wales, north of Sydney, Australia. Adventism in Australia has had a long history with John's gospel. A Bible institute organised at Avondale in 1896—even before the school officially opened—featured seminars on the Gospel of John by church administrator W W Prescott. His focus for the future faculty emphasised John's "I am" statements (for example, "I am the Good Shepherd") and its emphasis on the divinity of Christ.[9]

Almost 120 years later, Adventists in Australia continue to wrestle with the meaning of John's unique telling of the Jesus story. Carolyn Rickett, DArts, is a senior lecturer in Communication and English in the School of Humanities and Creative Arts. Daniel Reynaud, PhD, is dean of the Faculty of Arts and Theology, specialising in history, literature and media. Jane Fernandez, PhD, currently serves as the college's vice president for learning and teaching. Nathan Brown, book editor at Signs Publishing Company in Melbourne, Victoria (Australia), is an established author and currently a postgraduate student at Avondale.

What does a communications specialist who has written research articles on grief hear in the voices of Mary and Martha as they mourn their brother's death? How does a historian and literary scholar understand John's presentation of Jesus as he notices the repeated use of irony in the work? What does an academic administrator who has written on the psychology of violence see in the story of Jesus' encounter with a Samaritan woman? How does a senior graduate student used to editing the stories of others understand the footwashing scene found only in John's gospel?

The readings and responses of a variety of readers make the study of biblical texts an experience of abundant life. Readers of this book are encouraged to re-read John's gospel and consider their own presuppositions and perspectives. What do you see in the "signs" stories? What do you hear in the dialogues between Jesus and other characters? How do you follow John's use of irony?

Listening with the heart

In the years between the initial creation of these sermons and preparing them for publication, another important book shaped my appreciation of the complexities of John's gospel. For three years, from the beginning of 2002 to the end of 2004, 150 groups of people from many different walks of life, located in 22 countries, agreed to enter into a project together called "Through the Eyes of Another." The main question addressed in the project was: "What happens when Christians from radically different cultures and situations read the same Bible story and start talking about it with each other?"[10]

They agreed to read one scene of the New Testament—the story found in John 4 of the Samaritan woman Jesus met at a well. This story is a unique part of the narrative as it records the longest conversation between Jesus and any single person. This reading project was interested in what happens when people read and interpret a passage, then interact with other groups doing the same thing. Since stories always invite readers to "fill in the gaps" and readers do this from personal life experiences, what happens when readers do this in conversation with each other?

It is moving to hear the reports of this project. There are many ways in which our cultural assumptions, including our faith communities, shape how we hear and interpret the stories of Scripture. "We learned to listen with the heart," stated one participant.[11] "Looking through the eyes of another is not simple, but it is a very exciting and challenging search. It requires courage and openness. We are practising this as best we can, in the footsteps of Jesus and the Samaritan woman."[12]

In this present book, the five of us who share our readings hope these reflections on reading John's gospel, his account of Jesus' encounter with the Samaritan woman and his narrating of Jesus' seven signs will both exhibit and inspire "listening with the heart." As Seventh-day

Adventist women and men, we bring particular questions to these stories. As does each reader. It is our prayer that as you listen in on our conversations about how we read and respond to John's gospel that you, too, may find your own voice. Each new reading continues to enrich John's story of Jesus.

When we read in this way we also read with humility, understanding that new eyes will see new parts of the story. I am convinced of the wisdom of the literary theorist Mikhail Bakhtin, that it is in listening carefully to the voice of the other—respecting its true distinctive otherness—that we find our own voices.[13] This book is an occasion to consider our sacred texts as providing opportunities for hearing new voices, perhaps even our own. The questions for further reflection at the end of the book are designed to encourage more readings and more opportunities to respond to John's gospel.

The story of a book

Every book has its journey. As noted above, this book began life as a series of sermons on John's gospel. Each morning of that week in late March with its own signs of the arrival of Spring, I preached a sermon on a Johannine sign. Employees gathered in the large worship hall of the General Conference headquarters building. Following that series, I adapted the sermons and shared them with other congregations.

Five years later, I preached again from John—this time on "The Wedding at the Well"—in the Opal Room worship service at the Fox Valley Community Church in Wahroonga, New South Wales (Australia). A friend, Carolyn Rickett, who was with me that Autumn day, became enthused with a vision of what might be. Why not gather these sermons together in book form and make them more widely available to church members and local congregations? Perhaps, she also suggested, a CD could be included at the back of the book, providing a recorded version of the sermons. Also part of that first brainstorming session, our mutual friend, Robyn Priestley, joined in the many conversations that followed as we talked about how we could make it happen. As a result of those discussions, they wrote up a grant proposal to Avondale College to seek funding for the project. I am grateful to Carolyn and Robyn and to Avondale for the vision and resources that have made this book possible.

I am also grateful to students in my undergraduate "Jesus and the Gospels" classes over the past 20 years with whom I have read the Gospel of John. These classes have met on three different campuses: Columbia Union College (now Washington Adventist University) in Takoma Park, Maryland (USA); La Sierra University in Riverside, California (USA); and Avondale College. In addition, graduate courses in the Gospel of John that I taught at La Sierra University have further shaped my thinking and preaching, as has a recent course "Sacred Texts: Theory and Practice of New Testament Interpretation" where we read John's gospel from a variety of reader perspectives. Congregations from Brisbane, Queensland (Australia), to Sacramento, California (USA), to Markham Woods in Longwood, Florida (USA), have at various times invited me to share my reflections in a seminar series on John. Closer to my home in southern California, I am grateful to local church congregations who have shared a passion for Scripture as we read John's gospel together: Bonita Valley, Chino Hills Spanish, Corona and Loma Linda University.

John Brunt, senior pastor of the Azure Hills Seventh-day Adventist Church, and Kit Watts, retired associate editor of *Adventist Review*, read the seven sermons and offered encouragement as well as valuable suggestions for clarity. I am very grateful to both of them.

My parents, Bert and Mary Haloviak, have sat through this series of sermons more than once. In untold conversations over meals, they have expressed their love of John's gospel. My gratitude for their encouragement at each step of my journey with Scripture cannot be adequately expressed. They were present during the first delivery at the General Conference headquarters. Their prayers eased my nerves that week in 2004, and their enthusiastic responses each morning made it a week I will always remember.

My husband, Gil Valentine, aided in the transitioning of sermons to book chapters. It is a true gift to be able to share life with a writer who loves Scripture and these kinds of projects.

---

1. Ellen G White, *Selected Messages* Book I, Washington, DC: Review and Herald, 1958, page 17.

2. Wolfgang Iser, *The Act of Reading: A Theory of Aesthetic Response*, Baltimore, MD: Johns Hopkins University Press, 1978.

3. In our denominational tradition, we call this a "Week of Prayer." I am grateful to Dr Jan Paulsen, president of the General Conference of Seventh-day Adventists (1999-2010), for the invitation to speak for this series in March, 2004. The General Conference headquarters building is located in Silver Spring, Maryland (USA).

4. Takoma Park, Maryland: Review and Herald Publishing Association, 1975.

5. Paul N Anderson, *The Riddles of the Fourth Gospel: An Introduction to John*, Minneapolis, MN: Fortress Press, 2011.

6. The Fourth Gospel suggests that its author had access to many stories about Jesus and had to be very selective about the ones he chose to relate. See John 20:30, 31; 21:25.

7. The feeding of the 5000 is the only miracle found in all four canonical gospels (John 6:1–15; Matthew 14:14–21; Mark 6:32–44; Luke 9:12–17). The miracle at sea (John 6:16–21) is similar to miraculous events in Matthew 14:22–33; Mark 6:45–53; Luke 8:22–25.

8. Officially formed in 1863, the Seventh-day Adventist Church began as a Millerite Advent movement with its earliest members experiencing the "Great Disappointment" of 1844.

9. The sermons would later become a year-long series of Sabbath school lessons for the world church. For more information about Prescott's influence on Adventism in Australia, see Gilbert M Valentine, *W W Prescott: Forgotten Giant of Adventism's Second Generation*, Hagerstown, MD: Review and Herald, 2005, pages 111–30.

10. Hans de Wit, Louis Jonker, Marleen Kool, Daniel Schipani (editors), *Through the Eyes of Another: Intercultural Reading of the Bible*, Amsterdam: Institute of Mennonite Studies, 2004, page 4.

11. ibid, page 112.

12. ibid, page 81.

13. This value of the other's voice is a key idea for Bakhtin. In the context of encounters between different people and cultures, Bakhtin writes: "Each retains its own unity and open totality, but they are mutually enriched." See his "Response to a Question from the *Novy Mir* Editorial Staff" in *Speech Genres & Other Late Essays*, edited Caryl Emerson and Michael Holquist, translated Vern W McGee, Austin, TX: University of Texas Press, 1986, page 7. Bakhtin's convictions concerning the responsibilities of readers to respond to literature comes through in his famous statement ("Art and Answerability" in *Art and Answerability: Early Philosophical Essays* by M M Bakhtin, edited by Michael Holquist and Vadim Liapunov, translated by Vadim Liapunov, University of Texas Press Slavic Series, No 9, Austin, TX: University of Texas Press, 1990, page 1): "I have to answer with my own life for what I have experienced and understood in art, so that everything I have experienced and understood would not remain ineffectual in my life."

Part I

Signs To Life

A READER'S RESPONSE

Chapter 1

Signs of Salvation

John 2:1–11

In the Fourth Gospel's narrative of Jesus' life and ministry, characters first meet him through John the Baptist's proclamation (1:29–34). The next day people begin following Jesus and telling others about him (1:35–51). And "on the third day" the narrative highlights the first miracle performed by Jesus:

> On the third day there was a wedding in Cana of Galilee, and the mother of Jesus was there. Jesus and his disciples had also been invited to the wedding. When the wine gave out, the mother of Jesus said to him, "They have no wine." And Jesus said to her, "Woman, what concern is that to you and to me? My hour has not yet come." His mother said to the servants, "Do whatever he tells you." Now standing there were six stone water jars for the Jewish rites of purification, each holding twenty or thirty gallons. Jesus said to them [the servants], "Fill the jars with water." And they filled them up to the brim. He said to them, "Now draw some out, and take it to the chief steward." So they took it. When the steward tasted the water that had become wine, and did not know where it came from (though the servants who had drawn the water knew), the steward called the bridegroom and said to him, "Everyone serves the good wine first, and then the inferior wine after the guests have become drunk. But you

have kept the good wine until now." Jesus did this, the first
of his signs, in Cana of Galilee, and revealed his glory; and
his disciples believed in him (2:1–11).

Whenever I teach my "Jesus and the Gospels" class—a freshman-
level university course—I have my students read this story together.
The predictable question that arises in the minds of my 18-year-old
Adventist students is: "What's with the wine?"

One student—the kind who likes to get a heated discussion going—
can always be counted on to say something like: "This story shows that
it is OK to have wine with our meals." Another Adventist student will
then declare, "No, it does not! Jesus didn't make *alcoholic* wine!" And
the verbal battle is off and running. Students from other faith traditions
will shake their heads in wonder. Suddenly, a particularly Adventist
issue takes over a first-century story.

About the time John's gospel was written, another work not included
in the New Testament, called 2 Baruch, described the Messianic Age
as one when there will be plenty, including plenty of wine. In fact,
the work says that one of the signs of the Messianic Age will be that
each grape will yield the equivalent of 120 gallons (about 450 litres) of
wine.[1] We notice in the Cana wedding story how much water became
wine: at least 120 gallons—without even one grape!

John wanted his readers to understand that the Messianic Age had
arrived *in Jesus*. In him, there was an abundance of all that humanity
needed and desired. The writers of Baruch and the Fourth Gospel knew
that in the traditions of Israel, descriptions of a better future included
the presence of plenty of wine. The prophet Amos wrote about a time
when "mountains shall drip sweet wine and all the hills shall flow with
it" (Amos 9:13). Jesus' presence in Cana created an abundance of wine.
The story concludes with this affirmation: "Jesus did this, the first of
his signs, in Cana of Galilee, and revealed his glory; and his disciples
believed in him" (John 2:11).

It isn't about the "signs"

In the gospels of Matthew, Mark and Luke, Jesus performed miracles
that proclaimed the in-breaking of the kingdom of God. By contrast, in
John's gospel, the miracles, referred to as "signs," revealed truth, not so

much about the kingdom itself, as about Jesus, the God of the kingdom. The signs in the Fourth Gospel focused on Jesus' glory, and they were meant to lead readers to reaffirm belief in him. When John came to the end of his gospel account, he took pains to explain to readers his purpose in writing out his story about these "signs" of Jesus. They are written, he noted significantly, "so that you may continue to *believe* that Jesus is the Messiah, the Son of God, and that through believing, you may have life in his name" (20:31). John's carefully selected "sign" stories are intended to focus the reader on Jesus in a particular way and for a particular purpose.[2]

The people in the stories who witnessed Jesus' signs, had one of three reactions:

- They refused to believe in him;

- They believed in the signs instead of in him; or,

- They believed in what the signs pointed to—that Jesus was indeed the Christ![3]

I think the second of these responses is the most challenging for contemporary readers. We might feel pity for those who refuse to believe and possibly assume we fall into the third group, those who believe in Jesus Christ. But the people in the second group—those who liked signs and wonders, although they did not really care to what they pointed— are not where the Jesus of John's gospel wanted his followers to be. They were intrigued with the signs as phenomena but did not understand—or perhaps even want to understand—the real purpose of the signs.

Imagine you are visiting a significant building in your city. After a few wrong turns, you see outside along the highway the sign that has the name of the building on it. Now imagine if, in your delight to find this sign, you pulled your car over onto the shoulder of the road close to the sign, and you sat there gazing at it. *What a well-designed, attractive sign,* you think to yourself. *I am finally here! I have always wanted to visit this place, meet the employees, tour the building and see the visitors' centre.*

But you have not arrived! You are merely at the sign, which points to another reality—and you have not seen anything yet. The whole point of that sign on the highway is something far greater than the sign itself, however well designed and attractive it might be.

The first miracle in the Fourth Gospel concluded with these words: "Jesus did this, the first of his signs, in Cana of Galilee, and revealed his glory; and his disciples believed *in him*" (John 2:11, emphasis supplied). In this first sign—and in all the signs of this gospel—some people rejected Jesus, some fixated on the sign itself, and still others saw Jesus' glory and came to believe in him. The author of this gospel longed for his readers to see beyond the signs to Jesus' glory, and to continue to believe.

When Seventh-day Adventists hear the word "signs," do we think about Jesus' glory in the way John wanted us to? Probably not. We are possibly more conditioned to think about flagship magazine titles such as *Signs of the Times* and focus on things like doom and gloom, destruction and disaster, war and violence.[4] Some Christians—including Adventist Christians—spend a lot of their time counting down these "signs" rather than focusing on the Jesus to whom they point. They experience fear and anxiety about the future, instead of the assurance and hope that breathes life throughout the Fourth Gospel. Let us not stop at the signs, but look through them to see the Saviour.

Continuing to believe

Although there is much debate about the particular kind of readers to which this gospel was first written, most scholars think it was written primarily for and within a community comprised of people who were already followers of Jesus. Most likely, the Fourth Gospel was not written to evangelise pagans or to make new Christians as much as it was to encourage the faith of those who *were already* believers.[5] Here is another way in which the Fourth Gospel has relevance to people who perhaps have been associated with a church group for a long time. Members of such a community might know well the oft-rehearsed stories of Scripture, the memory verses, the words of the confession or the fundamental beliefs. Some might still remember their early lines from the catechism or from their Pathfinder pledge![6] Mission stories inspire them as they listen each week. Some people may even recall being involved in annual fundraising campaigns for mission projects.[7] Many give regularly to charities, in addition to paying tithes and giving local church offerings. Such believers already know the story of Jesus and appreciate something of what it means to live as disciples.

Recall again the purpose statement at the end of the Fourth Gospel, which can be translated from the original language as "these [stories about signs] are written that you may *continue* to believe" (20:31). When John's first readers heard his gospel being read, they already knew about Jesus. So do many of John's contemporary readers. Many of us have read about Jesus' ability to cast out demons as told in Mark's gospel. We have heard the Sermon on the Mount from Matthew's account. We know about Jesus' miraculous birth as told in Luke. But the Fourth Gospel quickly invites us to experience a new encounter with Jesus. John invites us to look again, to look deeper, to look further and to see Jesus' glory in a more meaningful life-changing way. He wants us to be guided by his signs that point beyond any particular unusual or out-of-the-ordinary event, to the wonder of Jesus himself!

From its beginning, the Fourth Gospel hints at what is to come. As readers follow the first words of the gospel, they are being prepared for the rest. This gospel is the only one of the four that starts the story at creation: "In the beginning was the Word, and the Word was with God, and the Word was God. He was in the beginning with God. All things came into being through him, and without him not one thing came into being" (1:1–3a). The first chapter of this gospel associates the divine word at Creation with Jesus who came in the flesh of humanity: "And the Word became flesh and lived among us" (1:14a). Somehow he was the embodiment of the divine glory (1:14b).

John invites us to look again, to look deeper, to look further and to see Jesus' glory in a more meaningful life-changing way.

Occasionally those among whom Jesus grew up, lived and worked perceived this glory. The Fourth Gospel selected some of the stories about these occasions and called them "signs" because they pointed to the glory of God dwelling on earth! Jesus was the "Word," the creator of everything. Jesus was the "Word," the re-creator of everything. John invites his readers to see Jesus' creative power and transforming glory, that is, to see that he is able to make things new again.

While the first half of the Fourth Gospel emphasises the signs that point to Jesus, the second half of the Fourth Gospel is often referred to as the "book of glory." Beginning in Chapter 12, Jesus refers to being "lifted up." This phrase has a double-meaning in this gospel. Believers know Jesus will be lifted up on a cross, which Romans thought to be the lowest, most shaming event a person could experience. Yet believers also know that Jesus' moment of crucifixion will be his moment of glory and exaltation. An event of shame is transformed into an experience of glory. The event of suffering transformed into glory can be the experience of all who continue to believe.

Echoes of another story

The wedding-at-Cana story is one of the first stories in the Fourth Gospel. But for the careful reader, it is clear that there are some fascinating connections with one of the last stories in this gospel. As you listen or read the words of the last story, notice words that are also found in the wedding story:

> Meanwhile, standing near the cross of Jesus were his mother, and his mother's sister, Mary the wife of Clopas, and Mary Magdalene. When Jesus saw his mother and the disciple whom he loved standing beside her, he said to his mother, "Woman, here is your son." Then he said to the disciple, "Here is your mother." And from that hour the disciple took her into his own home. After this, when Jesus knew that all was now finished, he said (in order to fulfill the scripture), "I am thirsty." A jar full of sour wine was standing there. So they put a sponge full of the wine on a branch of hyssop and held it to his mouth. When Jesus had received the wine, he said, "It is finished." Then he bowed his head and gave up his spirit. Since it was the day of Preparation, the Jews did not want the bodies left on the cross during the Sabbath, especially because that Sabbath was a day of great solemnity. So they asked Pilate to have the legs of the crucified men broken and the bodies removed. Then the soldiers came and broke the legs of the first and of the other who had been crucified with him. But when they came to Jesus and saw that he was already dead, they did not break his legs.

18

Instead, one of the soldiers pierced his side with a spear, and at once blood and water came out (19:25b–34).

We should have noticed that there are words, images and characters mentioned both here and in the Cana story. In both scenes, Jesus' mother was present—the only two places in John's gospel where she enters the narrative. In both scenes, Jesus called her "woman." While this may sound strange, perhaps even harsh to our ears, and while unusual for a son to use of his mother, this term would probably have been understood as a term of respect or honour. It does not carry the disrespectful connotations it does in many cultures today.

Both wedding and death scenes briefly refer to Jesus' "hour." At Cana, Jesus lets his mother know that this is not his hour. Jesus will repeat this over and over again throughout the gospel: "My hour is not yet come" (2:4; 7:30; 8:20), until finally "the hour *has* come" (12:23, 27–36; 13:1; 17:1), the hour of the cross—his hour of greatest glory; the hour *God* is glorified. At the cross, Jesus made sure that his mother was cared for from "that hour."

Both scenes also involve liquid. In Cana, the wine had run out and Jesus brought it back with great abundance. The water jars previously used for purification would be filled with the best wine ever. There would be plenty for all! At the cross, the wine is sour.[8] The One who had created the best wine was thirsty and asking for water. But he was given sour wine instead. Part of the torture of crucifixion was the agony of the elements. Hanging, sometimes for days, in the heat of the day and in the cold of the night, the crucified person's suffering was excruciating. Jesus was thirsty. We are meant to notice the irony. The "Water of Life" was thirsty.[9]

Unique to the Fourth Gospel's account of the crucifixion is the symbolism of water flowing out when Jesus died. The water came from Jesus' side after he was stabbed with a spear (19:34). The water in the wedding story was used to fill up the jars for the Jewish rite of purification. In the crucifixion story, water flowed because Jesus was stabbed. The authorities wanted him dead early because of the Jewish rite of the Sabbath. The Jews said, "We must get him down before the sun sets"—and they misunderstood the cross, that it was his moment of greatest glory. The best came last. Once again water flowed from God, the source of all life.

Adventist Christians—among others—believe in baptism by immersion, a special ceremony typically taking place in worship services that is only possible through the presence of abundant water. What if we celebrated each baptism as a reminder of Jesus' first sign, that of the water of purification becoming the sign of the Messianic Age?

When we celebrate baptisms, we also remember that water flowed from Jesus' side, that it "cleanses us from all sin." It is a sign of abundance and the sign of a glorious future. Each baptism is a beginning, the beginning of a future that breaks into the present and transforms the now. But it is also a reminder that Jesus saves the best for last! Each baptism is an invitation for disciples to believe once again: "Jesus did this, the first of his signs, in Cana of Galilee, and revealed his glory; and his disciples believed in him" (2:11).

"On the third day . . ."

Notice the way this wedding-at-Cana story began: "On the third day there was a wedding in Cana of Galilee . . ." Imagine being a Christian living at the time John was writing his gospel—toward the end of the first century—and hearing the phrase "On the third day . . ." This was a familiar phrase for early Christians. A listener to this gospel would be reminded immediately of Jesus' resurrection! Even as the author is setting up the story of this first sign, he is suggesting an anticipation of the final story about resurrection and re-creation. The scene here at the wedding concludes with the "glory" of Jesus being revealed and the "disciples believed in him."

This link in the Fourth Gospel also connects back to creation as events become infused with symbolic meaning. In the book of Genesis, the first three days of creation celebrate God's creation of light and water. Then, when living creatures had all they needed to survive, God created human beings on the sixth day. At the cross, on another "sixth day," humanity was re-created as water flowed out from the "light of the world."

On the third day, there was new life at Cana. It was the first of Jesus' signs. His glory was revealed and his disciples believed. And on another third day, the crucified One would have new life. It would be the most amazing sign of all. Jesus would be revealed in all his glory. But would his disciple believe in him? Would the first readers of the Fourth Gospel believe in him? Will contemporary readers believe in him?

1. 2 Baruch 29:5; see discussion by Raymond E Brown, *The Gospel According to John I–XII*, The Anchor Bible series, Garden City, NY: Doubleday & Company Inc, 1966, page 105.

2. Richard Manly Adams, Jr, in "Jesus did Many Other Signs: Aelius Aristides' Parchment Books and the Fourth Gospel's View of History" (paper presentation, Society of Biblical Literature Annual Meeting, San Francisco, California, November 22, 2011), compares Aristides' approach to history and audience to the Fourth Gospel's author. The author of the Fourth Gospel may have been suggesting that the miracles happened in the past, but the ones he selected to elaborate on were in order to help the current reader believe.

3. For example, see discussion by Raymond E Brown in "Appendix III," *The Gospel According to John I–XII*, op cit, pages 530-531. Susan E Hylen, *Imperfect Believers: Ambiguous Characters in the Gospel of John*, Louisville, KY: Westminster/John Knox Press, 2009, challenges this typical approach by suggesting that the majority of characters in this gospel are complex characters and therefore unable to be neatly categorised.

4. *Signs of the Times* magazine is familiar to most Seventh-day Adventists as highlighting the horrible happenings in our world as signs of the soon return of Jesus to fix all that is so very wrong.

5. There is debate over which manuscripts should be followed for this verse. Some translate the verb as an aorist subjunctive ("that you may believe"), others as a present subjunctive ("that you may keep believing"). The debate has ramifications for the purpose of this gospel: was it primarily a missionary tract or to strengthen the faith of those already believing in Jesus as the Christ? It seems to me that the best arguments are on the side of a present subjunctive translation.

6. Pathfinders is an Adventist youth organisation where young people are encouraged to integrate faith, learning, social activities and positive community involvement.

7. For Adventists it was "Ingathering," when all family members, including children, were

encouraged to participate in these fundraising initiatives on behalf of those living in poverty in the world.

8. Some translations use the word "vinegar," as it is a different Greek word from the one used in the Cana story.

9. See discussion in next chapter on John 4.

Chapter 2

A Wedding at the Well

John 4:4–42

Soon after the story of a wedding and drinking miraculous supplies of abundant wine, the author of the Fourth Gospel leads his reader into another intriguing encounter with Jesus centred on drinking. And in a subtle but surprising way, the reader is introduced to another discussion of miracles at weddings. This chapter is the only one in this part of the book that does not directly consider one of the Fourth Gospel's seven signs. However, like the other sign stories, this story of the Samaritan woman's encounter with Jesus also points to the future—to the cross and beyond—that breaks into the present.

The story contains so many symbolic connections to the other signs that it seems appropriate to include reflections on it here. This chapter, then, listens in on the conversation Jesus had with the Samaritan woman, and reflects on it in light of other encounters at wells and in light of the seven signs found in this gospel. The story of the Samaritan woman falls between the first sign, Jesus turning water into wine, and the second sign, the healing of a little boy (see John 4:46–54).

Of wells and weddings

Abraham had decided it was time for his son Isaac to get married. In Bible times, fathers decided such things. So Abraham sent his servant to go to the place of Abraham's birth, to a foreign land, to find a wife for Isaac among his relatives. The servant loaded 10 camels with lots of goods and gifts, and headed out.

After entering the foreign land, the servant stopped by a well and prayed. He said to God, "There are young women coming to this well to draw water. I am going to ask for a drink. May the one who gives me a drink and offers to water my camels be the wife you have chosen for Isaac." Before he finished his prayer, Rebekah arrived at the well and did everything he had asked. When she finished watering the camels, she ran home. The servant of Abraham was then invited to supper. But before he allowed himself to eat, he asked that arrangements be made for the marriage of Rebekah and Isaac (see Genesis 24).

Some years later, Isaac and Rebekah's son Jacob also met his bride at a well. After travelling to a foreign land, Jacob stopped near a well and began asking if anyone knew his relatives. Just then a young woman came up to the well. Her name was Rachel. Scripture says that Jacob kissed her and wept. Like Rebekah, her soon-to-be mother-in-law, Rachel immediately ran home. Eventually her father and Jacob made marriage arrangements (see Genesis 29).

Fast-forward in biblical history to the story of Moses. After Moses got into serious trouble with Egypt's pharaoh, Moses fled from Egypt and went into a foreign land called Midian. Scripture says that he "sat down by a well" (Exodus 2:15). As readers might expect, Moses met a woman at the well. In fact, the priest of Midian had seven daughters and they all came to the well where Moses rested, bringing their father's flocks to the water. But a group of shepherds started giving the women trouble. Moses stepped in, defended the women, made sure their flocks had all the water they needed, and then the women went to their home. After Moses was invited to supper, one of the seven sisters, Zipporah, was given to Moses in marriage (see Exodus 2).

Wells and weddings seem to go together.[1] Given this literary tradition, what would the first readers of the Fourth Gospel—especially those who knew Israel's stories—have understood about the scene that begins: "[Jesus] came to a Samaritan city called Sychar, near the plot of ground that Jacob had given to his son Joseph. Jacob's well was there, and Jesus, tired out by his journey, was sitting by the well. It was about noon [the sixth hour]" (4:5, 6)?

Like his ancestors, Jesus goes to a foreign land—to Samaritan land—and he sat down at a well. Could it be that the author of the Fourth Gospel is setting his readers up to think that Jesus was looking for a wife? For those who knew the stories of Isaac and Rebekah, Jacob and Rachel, Moses and Zipporah, it seemed to be exactly what Jesus was doing.

The story continues with what readers may have already anticipated: "A Samaritan woman came to draw water" (4:7). Just like Rebekah, just like Rachel, just like Zipporah and her sisters, a Samaritan woman came to the well. "And Jesus said to her: 'Give me a drink.' (His disciples had gone to the city to buy food)" (4:7, 8). Later in the story, when the disciples returned from getting food, they were surprised. The Fourth Gospel says that they "marvel that he is speaking with a woman." They wanted to ask—but did not—"What are you seeking?" or "What are you saying to her?" (4:27).

Just like Rebekah, just like Rachel, just like Zipporah and her sisters, a Samaritan woman came to the well.

Given their questions, the disciples seemed to assume that what happened at past wells was also going on at this one. Probably, given their understanding of the Messiah as an earthly ruler, Jesus seeking a wife was not a bad thing. But this particular woman was a huge problem! A Samaritan cannot be part of Jesus' family. She was *not* an acceptable bride.

After Jesus asked for a drink, the Fourth Gospel gives a clue when the woman replied: "'How is it that you, a Jew, ask a drink of me, a woman of Samaria?' Jews do not share things in common with Samaritans" (4:9). She was surprised Jesus was even talking to her. Women and men who were strangers did not talk together in public. She was more surprised that a Jew was asking her for a drink because Jews would not use a drinking vessel or an eating utensil that a Samaritan had used. Jews considered Samaritans unclean in every way.

Samaritans and other outsiders

It went back to a time of war, when those living in the land of Judah were conquered and relocated. Many of those who had stayed behind intermarried with other cultures and those who had not intermarried looked down on these Samaritans. Many wars produce bi-racial children, with one parent from the invading nation and the other parent from the conquered nation. Through no fault of their own, the children are usually despised by both ethnic groups.

Today, we should ask what group of people is a contemporary equivalent to first-century Samaritans. Whose cup would we refuse? Who is "dirty"? Those begging near the off-ramp of the highway? The sunburned woman talking to herself in front of the grocery store? The mother in the check-out line who seems like she could abuse her children? Racists? Sexists? Terrorists? For some—even some calling themselves Christians—people from different racial, ethnic or religious groups are the "dirty" people. For some, the "dirty ones" are the religious "liberals" or "conservatives" within their own faith community. Whose cup would we refuse?

From the disciples' perspective, the Samaritan woman was an untouchable. She cannot be part of Jesus' family. They probably wondered why Jesus did not hang out more at wells back in Galilee or around Jerusalem. That was where reputable Jewish men found future kin—not in Samaria. Every minute that Jesus talks with her is a violation of appropriate social behaviour—yet Jesus keeps talking! It turns out to be the longest conversation Jesus has with any one individual in the entire Fourth Gospel. This is not a part of the narrative to skip over.

Stepping into her story

Jesus continued by saying to her:

> "If you knew the gift of God, and who it is that is saying to you, 'give me a drink,' you would have asked him, and he would have given you living water." The woman said to him, "Sir, you have no bucket, and the well is deep. Where do you get that living water? Are you greater than our ancestor Jacob, who gave us the well, and with his sons and his flocks drank from it?" (4:10–12).

26

This part of the discourse includes a reference to Jacob, reminding readers of the narrator's voice that earlier linked this story with Jacob's story (4:5, 6). We are reminded that Jacob was born because of an encounter at a well. Jacob became the father of a dozen sons and at least one daughter because of an encounter at a well. Jacob and his sons used this water supply to care for their fields and provide for their animals. The Samaritan woman asked Jesus: "Are you greater than Jacob?"

I imagine the writer of this gospel grinning as he wrote this part. His gospel began: "In the beginning was the Word . . . and the Word was with God, and the Word was God!" Was Jesus greater than Jacob? Jacob gave his sons—the Samaritan woman's ancestors—this well and its water supply; a secure place to live and flourish. Jacob gave her ancestors a future. What about Jesus? Was Jesus greater than Jacob?

But Jesus avoids giving a direct reply to the question. Instead, he describes what he could do for her. He responded cryptically: "Everyone who drinks of this water will be thirsty again, but those who drink of the water that I will give them will never be thirsty. The water that I will give will become in them a spring of water gushing up to eternal life'" (4:13, 14).

> **I imagine the writer of this gospel grinning as he wrote this part.**

"Sir, give me this water," she replied.

Jesus' next words surprise me. To be honest, they disappoint me. Immediately after she asked him for the water, Jesus said: "Go get your husband."

Why did Jesus bring up her past? She had progressed from assuming that her ancestor Jacob was greater than Jesus to asking Jesus for living water. That is what people are supposed to do when they encounter Jesus, right? In the other gospels, whenever someone said, "Help me, Jesus," he did. In the other gospels, whenever someone said, "If you are willing, you can make me clean," Jesus responded, "I am willing." He always gave people a new, clean start. So why did Jesus bring up her past?

Many of us tend to think of the Samaritan woman as a loose woman with a sinful past. When we hear of five marriages and that she then lived with a man who was not her husband, we assume she had made a lot of poor choices in life. However, in the world of Jesus' day, men decided issues of marriage and divorce, not women. Only husbands could get a divorce, abandon their families or kick out their spouse. At the same time, women could not survive unless they were attached to a man. After this woman's first abandonment—through death or divorce—if she did not have a father, brother or son who would take her in, she *had* to attach herself to another man in order to survive. Going through this experience five times was tragic beyond words. Given the world of Jesus' day, her story was probably more of a discarded woman with a painful past, rather than that of a loose woman with a sinful past.

Since her current living conditions were based on her own survival, she was living with someone who refused to acknowledge his responsibility to her. She was probably more of a slave who had to do whatever he wanted, than a secret lover having an affair. She was trying to survive. He should have married her.

Whatever her sad story—in society's view, as well as in her own mind—this woman was as different from Rebekah, Rachel and Zipporah as it was possible for her to be. *They* were young virgins with fathers who offered security prior to a proper marriage. They met men who, guided by God, offered the protection of a home, the promise of children and the hope of a future. This Samaritan woman did not seem to have any of these things. Hers was a painful past, a sad present and an uncertain future.

For all who can relate to her story, Jesus sits at the well. Yes, he is greater than Jacob. Jesus provides a new kind of water, and a secure place to live and flourish. Jesus gives the hope for a future.

"Come and see"

For the first time in this gospel, Jesus shares his true identity. When the Samaritan woman began talking about the Messiah who *is coming,* Jesus said: "I am." Her hope for the future was also for the present! The Messiah was no longer something to anticipate. The Messiah was present with her, sitting at the well.

Typically in Old Testament scenes when women and men met at wells, the woman left and went home to her family, then her family came out to meet the man at the well, the future bridegroom. Then, in sharing a meal, the two families made wedding plans.

However, in John 4, the Samaritan woman did not go to her family. This is another clue that she probably did not have one. But she did go to her community. The Fourth Gospel's interest in directional movement almost feels humorous when it describes that she went *to* town in order to tell everyone about the Messiah, as the disciples arrived *from* town with food for Jesus.

But Jesus refused the food. Instead Jesus began talking about his food being the completion of God's work (4:31–38). Recall that Abraham's servant refused to eat anything until he had completed the marriage arrangements between Isaac and Rebekah. Jesus refused to eat what the disciples brought from town. Instead, Jesus had wedding plans to arrange, as if such plans are God's work!

The disciples were confused, wondering who gave Jesus food when they were not looking. Meanwhile, the Samaritan woman was preaching her heart out in the town. She did what the first disciples did when they witnessed to Jesus earlier in the gospel: "Come and see," she says. "Come and see"! (4:29, compare 1:46). She was an apostle—and people in her town come to believe in Jesus "because of her word" (4:39, 42, compare 17:20).

> The Fourth Gospel's interest in directional movement almost feels humorous when it describes that she went *to* town in order to tell everyone about the Messiah, as the disciples arrived *from* town with food for Jesus.

What got a town of Samaritans interested in a thirsty Jewish man sitting by a well? Jesus did not have 10 camels loaded with goods and gifts. Jesus did not even have a bucket! Somehow her message brought them. Perhaps the best mission a local congregation can embrace is to simply be a place where people are invited to "come and see." People with painful pasts speak with authenticity and power when *they* say, "Come and see."

While Jesus was talking about fields ripe for harvest, the disciples were puzzled. They went into the city and brought back food that Jesus refused. It had not occurred to them to bring back people—in order to plan a wedding!

In an important way, the Samaritan woman was like her foremothers Rebekah, Rachel and Zipporah. She made possible the joining of two families! As Jesus kept talking about the fields ripe for harvest, the people from the town started coming across those fields in order to meet Jesus at the well. They would share a meal with him—a real meal with Jesus' true food, which was to do God's will, to share God's goodness with Samaritans and create a new family.

Together they will make marriage plans. The Fourth Gospel says that Jesus "remained" with them for two days. It is the same word used by the Fourth Gospel to describe how the Spirit "remained" with Jesus after his baptism (1:32, 39). The language suggests intimacy, connection and kinship. They joined together as one family.

Staying for two days meant sharing a lot of eating utensils and drinking vessels! What boundaries were broken down during those two days? When women from other Samaritan homes went to the well for water to cook and serve Jesus and his disciples, did the disciples go with them to help? How were the disciples' eyes opened? After all, in the future that unfolded following Jesus' death and resurrection, Jesus' disciples—following the Samaritan woman's example—brought all kinds of people to Jesus.

Other stories, other signs

The story of this encounter between Jesus and this woman at a Samaritan well reminded readers of the first sign, when Jesus created a miracle at a wedding. Jesus' discussion about thirst and "drawing water" brought to mind the water transformed in Cana. The woman's water jar recalled the six stone water jars used for purification. But she did not need her jar anymore—in fact, she left it behind in her excitement about her good news. Both stories involved women—Mary, Jesus' mother, and the Samaritan woman. Both women gained insights into Jesus and his identity. In both stories, Jesus' disciples understood Jesus in new ways, too. And both stories report amazing transformations: of wine and weddings, women, even whole towns.

At the end of John's gospel, when Jesus was handed over to be crucified, it was said to be "the sixth hour" (noon)—the same time that Jesus rested at the well and met the Samaritan woman (4:6, compare 19:13, 14). If we might extend the artistry of the narrative, imagine her story and her voice suddenly joining others at the cross:

> Jesus said, "I'm thirsty" (19:28)—and she might respond: "I now know that you would drink after me, using a Samaritan's cup."

> Jesus said, "I'm thirsty"—and she might respond: "I left my jar at the well. I didn't realise I would need it again, that *you* of all people would need it."

> Jesus said, "I'm thirsty"—and she might reply: "But you *are* the Living Water."

> Jesus said, "I'm thirsty"—and she would ask: "What are you thirsty for, Jesus?"

Are you thirsty for a world where Jews and Samaritans worship together? Are you thirsty for a world where justice and righteousness flow like streams, like living water? Are you thirsty for a world where women with painful pasts can experience security in a new type of family? Are you thirsty for a world without prejudice and without discrimination? Are you thirsty for a world without crucifixions and all other kinds of violence? Are you thirsty for a world where women and men meet at wells and offer each other a future with integrity and intimacy, loyalty and love? Are you thirsty for a world where people of all nations make up your family? Are you thirsty for a world where no-one is ever thirsty again?

Jesus' last words from the cross declared, "It is finished." Among other things, the barriers between a Jewish man and a Samaritan town were finished. They were one family. The Fourth Gospel says that a soldier "pierced Jesus' side with a spear, and at once blood and water came out" (19:34). Jacob's well provided water for the fields of Sychar, but the water from Jesus' side nourished a world of fields ripe for harvest— lands waiting for harvesters.

What might it mean to live in such a way that the Living Water bubbles up in us? What might it mean if sharing that Living Water with

31

others was our nourishment, our food? Imagine people in *our* towns saying to us in the words that forever honour the Samaritan woman: "It is no longer because of what you said that we believe, for we have heard for ourselves, and we know that this is truly the Saviour of the world" (4:42).

1. Robert Alter, *The Art of Biblical Narrative*, New York: Basic Books, 1981, pages 55–8, discusses this type-scene.

Chapter 3

Belief Before Signs

John 4:46–54

n Chapter 1, we explored the meaning of the first sign performed by Jesus in John's gospel, when Jesus turned more than 450 litres (120 gallons) of water into wine, while attending a wedding. According to the Fourth Gospel's order of events, Jesus then undertook a journey by foot of more than 140 kilometres (90 miles) in order to get to Jerusalem and participate in the Passover festival. While he was there in Jerusalem, John tells us, "Many believed in his name because they saw the signs that he was doing" (2:23).

We also saw that characters in John's gospel who witnessed a sign by Jesus have one of three reactions: they refused to believe in him; they remained focused on the signs instead of him; or they believed in what the signs pointed to—Jesus the Christ. This third group saw the glory of God shining through the sign. In the story about Jesus' second sign, John added a fourth category of response: there were some who believed in Jesus even before they witnessed a sign! These kinds of people represented those who were willing to believe in Jesus *because of his word*.

While still in Jerusalem, John tells us, Jesus experienced a midnight encounter with a Jewish man named Nicodemus (3:1–21). As Jesus left Jerusalem, he took the long way home. First, Jesus went across the Jordan, where baptisms were taking place (3:22–24). Then he went through Samaria where he had a noon-day encounter with a Samaritan woman and then the people of her village (4:4–26, 39–42).

Back in Cana

When Jesus finally arrived back in the region of the Galilee, John tracks him again to Cana where he now performs his second sign. The scene began with a reminder to readers of the earlier miracle, then shifts to a discussion of the new need. Notice the way John relates the sequence:

> Then he came again to Cana in Galilee where he had changed the water into wine. Now there was a royal official whose son lay ill in Capernaum. When he heard that Jesus had come from Judea to Galilee, he went and begged him to come down and heal his son, for he was at the point of death (4:46, 47).

A "royal official" was no ordinary person. This man was probably part of the household of Herod Antipas. At the time of Jesus, Herod Antipas—son of Herod the Great—was ruler of the region of the Galilee, a mountainous territory of about 3000 square kilometres (1200 square miles) with numerous fertile valleys. This royal official's son was very sick. Readers are not told the son's age, but a word used later in the story (verse 49) suggests the child is quite young.

When a child is ill, everything else takes second place for parents. If medication is needed in the middle of the night, sleep is sacrificed. An emergency visit to a medical facility during working hours means that heavy work responsibilities are immediately set aside. Exhausted parents stay up all night to bring down a fever or to stay alert beside a hospital bed. The health of the child becomes the central focus of their lives.

This official from Herod's court made the 13-kilometre (8-mile) uphill climb from Capernaum, near the sea of Galilee, to Cana: "When he heard that Jesus had come from Judea to Galilee, he went and begged him to come down and heal his son, for he was at the point of death" (4:47). Typically in the gospel accounts, when a person begged Jesus for healing, Jesus responded immediately. But in this case, Jesus did something surprising. Jesus said to this worried father: "Unless you see signs and wonders you will not believe" (verse 48).

Why does John have Jesus respond to the father with such strange, almost-hostile words? It seems Jesus was looking over the shoulder of the father to the crowd beyond. In the original language, it is clear that Jesus did not respond directly to the father, because the pronoun translated as "you" is in the plural form. Jesus spoke to more than one person when he said: "Unless you *people* see signs and wonders you will not believe."

Was Jesus still upset about those in Jerusalem who believed only in the signs? Was Jesus concerned that the people in Galilee would also respond in this way? Since he had returned home, had people been asking for more "wine-miracles"?

But this father would not back down. He was neither distracted nor offended by Jesus' comment to the crowd. As John relates the story, "The official said to him, 'Sir, come down before my little boy dies.' Jesus said to him, 'Go; your son will live.' The man believed the word that Jesus spoke to him and started on his way" (4:50).

It seems as if the whole exchange had taken place in just four sentences. Of course, the conversation may have taken much longer than this but John captures the essence of it. According to the Fourth Gospel, this fourth category of response was the best possible response! This response was how the writer of the gospel wanted every reader to respond: to believe the words of Jesus, even before witnessing a sign. Readers were to believe and then start on their way.

Receiving life

Jesus told the man of the court that his son would live, and the little boy received *life*. This is a word pregnant with meaning and vitally important throughout John's gospel.

This is the gospel—the only gospel—in which Jesus said: "I have come that they may have *life*, and have it more abundantly" (10:10). This is the gospel—the only gospel—in which Jesus proclaimed: "I am the way, and the truth, and the life" (14:6). This is the gospel—the only gospel—where Jesus prayed: "This is eternal life, that they may know you, the only true God, and Jesus Christ whom you have sent" (17:3).

This gospel includes the unique story of Nicodemus who was told to be born again in order to experience life in the Spirit and that "God so loved the world that he gave his only son, so that everyone who believes in him may not perish but may have eternal *life*" (3:16). This is the gospel where the Samaritan woman at the well was told about "living

35

water" (4:10) and that "the water that [Jesus] will give will become . . .
a spring of water gushing up to eternal *life*" (4:14).

In this nine-verse story of Jesus' second sign, the story of a worried
father and a very sick little boy, the word "life" appears three times:

> Jesus said to him, "Go; your son will *live*." The man believed
> the word that Jesus spoke to him and started on his way. As
> he was going down, his slaves met him and told him that his
> child was *alive*. So he asked them the hour when he began
> to recover, and they said to him, "Yesterday at one in the
> afternoon the fever left him." The father realised that this was
> the hour when Jesus had said to him, "Your son will *live*." So
> he himself believed, along with his whole household. Now
> this was the second sign that Jesus did after coming from
> Judea to Galilee (4:50–54).

Another word that is repeated three times in these few verses is the
word "hour." Unlike most English translations that describe the time of
the boy's recovery as "one in the afternoon," the phrase "seventh hour" is
used in the original language. The repetition is powerful: the royal official
asked the *hour* his son recovered (4:52), and the servants responded,
"the seventh *hour*" (4:52), and then the father realised that that was
the very *hour* Jesus had said, "Your son will live" (4:53). This repetition
reminded careful readers of Jesus' earlier words in Cana: "My hour has
not yet come" (2:4). This second miracle in Cana—the hour of the boy's
recovery—was tied to Jesus' own "hour," an "hour" that had not yet come.
It is unmistakably clear. This second miracle is presented by the author as
a sign pointing to Jesus' hour, specifically his hour on the cross.

According to the Fourth Gospel, the hour of Jesus' most amazing sign
was the hour that made possible the recovery of all creation! Every sick
boy and girl, every worried father and stressed-out mother can know
the hour of their recovery: when Jesus' hour arrived.

Believing before seeing

It is important to note that the father believed *before* he saw the sign.
He believed at the *beginning* of his journey home, not only when he
met his slaves and hugged his boy. In this way, the royal official father
becomes an example for all John's readers.

I am an "I'll-believe-it-when-I-see-it" kind of person. Because I do not like the label "skeptic," I typically use the word "realistic" to describe this characteristic. A friend once told me about a major financial donation that had been pledged for a church institution I care deeply about. I remember that my immediate response was: "I'll believe it when I see the cheque. No, wait, I'll believe it when the cheque is deposited and the money shows up on the bank statement!" My friend was understandably taken aback by my reaction. He wanted me to join him in celebrating this promised gift. A heart that believes "only when I see it" is a heart that will miss seeing so much of the life-giving truth this gospel shares with its readers.

The Fourth Gospel invites us to a life of believing *even before* seeing. It invites us to begin walking home, *before* we witness the wonder. We are to start on our way, before we see the sign. It is such an important insight that the author wants his readers to understand that he brings us back to the point at the end of his story about Jesus.

Responding in the only way appropriate to the situation, Thomas declares, "My Lord and my God!" (20:28).

At the end of the Fourth Gospel—after Jesus' resurrection—John narrates an encounter between the risen Christ and some of the disciples. However, the disciple Thomas was absent.

When the others tell Thomas about their experience of seeing Jesus, Thomas responds: "Unless I see the mark of the nails in his hands, and put my finger in the mark of the nails and my hand in his side, I will not believe" (20:25). In effect, Thomas said, "I'll believe it when I see it."

Suddenly, with all the doors shut, Jesus appeared in the house where Thomas and his fellow disciples had gathered. Jesus looked directly at Thomas and said, "Put your finger here and see my hands. Reach out your hand and put it in my side. Do not doubt, but believe" (20:27). Responding in the only way appropriate to the situation, Thomas declares, "My Lord and my God!" (20:28).

Then, for the last time in this twentieth chapter—a chapter many people believe was the original conclusion of this gospel—Jesus said:

"Have you believed because you have seen me? Blessed are those who have not seen and yet have come to believe" (20:29).

Should readers remember the royal official? Should contemporary readers think about themselves? "Blessed are those who have not seen and yet have come to believe."

The Fourth Gospel does not contain a "Sermon on the Mount" with beatitudes like Matthew and Luke, but it does contain this beatitude— or blessing—"Blessed are those who have not seen and yet have come to believe."

But what if the one reading Jesus' blessing is one whose faith has grown thin lately? What if she is barely a believer these days? What if his questions have pushed faith away? What if their tears have extinguished their hope? Such readers find encouragement in the actions of the royal official. What did he do as a believer? He headed home.

He did not become a disciple, in the sense of leaving house and family to follow Jesus. He did not set up evangelistic meetings on the shore of the Sea of Galilee. He did not start trying to perform healing miracles himself. He just headed home. And, along the way, his faith was strengthened, first, through a verbal telling of the sign. Then his faith was strengthened more when he saw his healthy son. Then his faith was strengthened even more when he told his family about his encounter with Jesus, a simple but strange encounter. Then his faith was strengthened more when his family came to believe (4:53).

Believing together

In the Fourth Gospel, faith is a moving toward Jesus, a process of coming to see who he is and a willingness to notice the signs that point to him. For John, this faith process was not a solo experience. It was not about people having to figure out how to have more faith. Instead, this gospel suggests that *people* and their stories help others in their believing.

When Jesus called his first disciples, Andrew helped his brother Peter, and Philip helped Nathaniel (1:40–42, 43–45). Jesus helped Nicodemus and the Samaritan woman at the well. Then the Samaritan woman helped the people of her village. The royal official's slaves helped him, and then the royal official helped his family. And the stories continued.

Jesus helped his first disciples see, then their witness was written down eventually into gospels that help us (17:20).

While I was attending seminary and serving as associate pastor of the All Nations Church just near the seminary, I experienced something I will never forget one day at worship. David, one of our parishioners, got up to sing the special music. David had recently experienced a terrible loss. After beginning to sing, his voice broke and he had to start over. The congregation encouraged him—"That's OK," several called out—and David began again.

But it was just too difficult. David stood on the platform, the pianist playing the song, but his voice was less and less able to form sounds. Tears were beginning to fall down his face. Suddenly the most amazing thing happened. Carlton—another church member at All Nations—who was sitting in the middle of the congregation, picked up the song with his strong, clear voice. As he sang, he gradually made his way to the platform until he joined David, placing his arm around David's shaking shoulders.

There they stood: one singing, one unable to sing. They were two men who had grown up in different parts of the world. Their first languages were different. Their clothing and hairstyles were different. But they

Through the experience of caring for each other, the faith of each of us will be strengthened. Disciples help each other believe.

were brothers in faith and in hope. When the song ended, we all knew we had already heard and seen the sermon that day—a sermon about what it means to be church and to grow in faith through the faith of others.

Perhaps today you cannot sing—it is just too difficult—but the rest of us can hold you up. And through the experience of caring for each other, the faith of each of us will be strengthened. Disciples help each other believe.

In Jesus' prayer of John 17, he first prayed on behalf of his disciples, then for those who would experience the disciples' witness: "I ask not only on behalf of these, but also on behalf of those who will believe in me through their word" (17:20). Jesus prayed on behalf of *all* believers. He prayed for those who believed after seeing Jesus heal a little boy, *and* for those who believe after reading the story of the little boy and his worried father. Jesus prayed on behalf of those in Cana who believed after tasting the water that became wine, *and* for those who believed after hearing of abundant wine and of Jesus dying of thirst on a cross.

Jesus prays on behalf of all believers, including Thomas, the one who doubted. And all of us—those with great faith and those with faith that will barely get us through this day—respond in the only way appropriate: "My Lord and my God."

Chapter 4

The Sabbath as Sign

John 5:1-18

I enjoy visiting the city of Bethesda in Maryland, USA. It is a delightful town on the northwestern edge of Washington, DC, where the Maryland suburbs start. The downtown area includes a giant three-storey Barnes & Noble bookstore, distinctive restaurant choices and a delightful footpath that meanders along the Potomac River all the way to historic Georgetown.

Directly in front of the bookstore at Bethesda sits a large water fountain. Several stone ledges surround the water, where people can stop and rest. On one ledge sits part of the fountain display: a modern cane looking as if it were recently left at the fountain. It is so modern and real, pedestrians often try to pick it up and find the person who lost it. They are puzzled when it does not budge. It is firmly and cleverly embedded in the granite. However, those who know the Fourth Gospel—or see the plaque beside the fountain—understand this piece of downtown artwork: "There is a pool, called in Hebrew 'Bethesda'" (John 5:2). The abandoned cane is meant to remind people of a story that took place at *another* Bethesda.

The original Bethesda

The third sign found in the Fourth Gospel begins:

Now in Jerusalem by the Sheep Gate there is a pool, called

41

in Hebrew Bethesda, which has five porticoes. In these lay many invalids—blind, lame and paralysed. One man was there who had been ill for thirty-eight years. When Jesus saw him lying there and knew that he had been there a long time, he said to him, 'Do you want to be made well? (5:2–6).

Depending on how one pronounces the word, "Bethesda" can mean either a "house of mercy" or "Bet Esda," which means "house of the flowing."[1] Either way the word is pronounced, both phrases are appropriate for the story we read in John 5, since the pool of Bethesda was both a "house of mercy" where people left their sick loved ones hoping they would be cared for, as well as being a place with water that, perhaps, occasionally "flowed."[2]

A pool like the one described in John 5 has been discovered and excavated by archaeologists in Jerusalem. I have stood at the edge of what was once a pool, with porches around and stairs that descended from the porches into the pool. Archaeologists wonder if perhaps the pool was constructed above intermittent springs.

Verse 4 of our narrative is thought by most scholars to have been absent from the earliest forms of this gospel. Like a sidebar comment on the page of the text, it refers to a popular belief of the time concerning the healing power of the spring. The note explains that those who were sickly were "waiting for the stirring of the water; for an angel of the Lord went down at certain seasons into the pool, and stirred up the water; whoever stepped in first after the stirring of the water was made well from whatever disease that person had." So in the minds of the people of Jerusalem, Bethesda was a "house of mercy" and it was a "house of the flowing."

Into this place of the sick and dying, Jesus walked. The Fourth Gospel infuses the name of the place with new spiritual meaning. Only when Jesus arrived there did it truly became a "house of mercy." *His* presence made it a house flowing with the water of life.

The author of the Fourth Gospel is a careful and intentional writer. In the previous chapter of this gospel (4:6), we found Jesus visiting another place where there was water. I think John wants us to note that before going to a unique pool, Jesus stopped by an historic well. In his encounter with the Samaritan woman at the well near the village of Sychar—about 65 kilometres (40 miles) north of Jerusalem—Jesus gradually led her to embrace the conviction that she was talking to the Messiah.

The woman was surprised by many things. First, she was surprised that he—a Jew—was willing to drink from a Samaritan's drinking vessel (4:9). Second, she was surprised that this man—a stranger in town— knew where flowing water could be found (4:11, 12). She was also surprised that Jesus' water source did not require a bucket (4:11). Then she was surprised that somehow he had water that, when drunk, keeps one from ever getting thirsty again (4:13–15). She was also surprised that he knew about her past (4:19) and that he had unusual views about worship (4:20–25). Finally, she was surprised that Jesus stood before her and claimed to be the "I am." Jesus identified himself to her with this deeply meaningful phrase and it was the first time he did so in the Fourth Gospel (4:26).

When Jesus' disciples got back from town, it was their turn to be surprised. They were surprised to see that Jesus was talking publicly to a woman—a Samaritan woman at that![3] She went into her town and told everyone to "come and see" (4:29). She used an invitation *His* **presence made hers a house flowing with the water of life.** similar to the phrase used earlier in John's narrative by the disciple Philip when he witnessed to Nathanael (1:46). The description used here in the Fourth Gospel makes it clear to readers: this Samaritan woman is a disciple! She had drunk of the living water and it had become in her a "spring of water gushing up to eternal life" (4:14).

The Samaritan woman of John 4 found the living water. *His* presence made hers a house flowing with the water of life.

After 38 years

Now at Bethesda, there was a man dying of thirst. He was dried out, shrivelled with the waiting of 38 years, even while lying and living next to a pool. But it was a pool that could not help him. He desperately needed the living water. The story described Jesus as seeing the man lying there, knowing that the man had been there a long time. Then the narrative focuses on Jesus' question to the man: "Do you want to be made well?" (5:6).

Imagine going around a place where there are people who are sick and dying and asking, "Do you wish to be made well?" For six years while studying, I worked part-time as a nurse's aide at a local nursing home near my home town of Beltsville, Maryland. I can only imagine the looks I would have received had I asked the residents in my care, "Do you wish to be younger?" "Would you like your eyesight back?" "Would you appreciate strong limbs again, without arthritis?" "Would you like to hear perfectly without a hearing aid?" "How would you like to get around without this wheelchair or that walker?"

This man at Bethesda's pool had been there for 38 years. If it is true that the average life span for a male during Jesus' day was about 40 years, the crippled man had spent a lifetime at Bethesda's pool.

If we had our journalist's notepad in our pocket, we might have asked why the man had been brought and left at the "house of mercy" so long ago. Was it that, as a young child, his legs had not formed properly? Were his poor parents unable to keep a child who would never be able to work the fields? Was the disgrace too much? Did they think he had a better chance in the "house of mercy" than in their own tiny single-room mud house? Whatever his story—and we simply do not get to know the details—the crippled man had been at Bethesda's pool for 38 years and was now an old man.

Jesus asked him: "Do you wish to be made well?" Readers might have expected him to respond with an enthusiastic "Yes!" But the man never really replied to Jesus' question at all. Instead, he simply explained why he was still sick:

> The sick man answered [Jesus], "Sir, I have no-one to put me into the pool when the water is stirred up; and while I am making my way, someone else steps down ahead of me." Jesus said to him, "Stand up, take your mat and walk." At once the man was made well, and he took up his mat and began to walk. Now that day was a Sabbath (5:7–9).

It is worth noting that the Fourth Gospel does not give us any further details about how the man felt or exactly what had been fixed in the healing. The last part of verse nine hints ominously at the major issue of concern that becomes the focus of the rest of this story and the significance of this sign.

The troublesome Sabbath sign

The rest of the chapter moves on to explain how the first active hostility against Jesus reported in the Fourth Gospel arose. *This* sign is going to divide people, and those who refused to believe became Jesus' enemies throughout the rest of the narrative. *This* sign was going to get Jesus into trouble and the writer wants us to understand why. Therefore he explains at some length:

> So the Jews said to the man who had been cured, "It is the Sabbath; it is not lawful for you to carry your mat." But he answered them, "The man who made me well said to me, 'Take up your mat and walk.'" They asked him, "Who is the man who said to you, 'Take it up and walk'?" Now the man who had been healed did not know who it was, for Jesus had disappeared in the crowd that was there. Later Jesus found him in the temple and said to him, "See, you have been made well! Do not sin anymore, so that nothing worse happens to you" (5:10–14).

The reader is now perhaps wondering what is going on here. What is the backstory? What has this fellow been up to? But our storyteller is not distracted by that and does not want us to be. He presses on with his explanation about what happened next. The story continues:

> The man went away and told the Jews that it was Jesus who had made him well. Therefore the Jews started persecuting Jesus, because he was doing such things on the Sabbath. But Jesus answered them, "My Father is still working, and I also am working." For this reason the Jews were seeking all the more to kill him, because he was not only breaking the Sabbath, but was also calling God his own Father, thereby making himself equal to God (5:15–18).

Suddenly, we are into serious theology. The writer wants us to understand that Jesus got into trouble on two fronts: first, Jesus did not keep the Sabbath properly; and, second, Jesus was claiming divine status. The topic of God's actions during the Sabbath hours had caused much debate among the Jews in Jesus' day. Finally, it had been decided that God did work on the Sabbath. After all, it was work to sustain life: to send rain, to cause things to grow, to allow Sabbath births. Yes, God must work on the Sabbath—but that was defensible. God was the author of the Sabbath. But certainly, no human was to work.

Knowing of this debate and the reasoning it involved, Jesus responded as if he were saying, "Yes, it is perfectly appropriate that I healed the man at the pool during the Sabbath hours, because my Father and I work on the Sabbath. That is *precisely* how God keeps the Sabbath! God is about the business of creating and re-creating, healing bodies and restoring people to their communities." When Jesus gave this reply to his interrogators, readers learn for the first time that "the Jews" were trying to kill Jesus.[4]

In the span of just a few verses, the scene morphs from a stunning healing to outrage over Sabbath behaviour (5:10), to persecution (5:16) and then to plotted homicide (5:18). And "the Jews" felt justified about all this because Jesus was claiming to be God. Jesus was claiming the right to work during the Sabbath, just as God the Creator and Sustainer does not stop working on the Sabbath.

Those who read the Fourth Gospel through to its conclusion know that Jesus will keep doing the work of Creator, Sustainer and Restorer. Jesus will only rest on the Sabbath after his greatest work is completed, only after he utters his triumphant "It is finished" (19:30). But at this point in the story Jesus responded to his accusers, "Very truly, I tell you, the Son can do nothing on his own, but only what he sees the Father doing; for whatever the Father does, the Son does likewise" (5:19). Jesus does not back away from the interpretation that his Jewish listeners have given to his words. He does not dispute their conclusions. In fact, John has him saying even more. He strengthens their assertions, when he continues:

> The Father loves the Son and shows him all that he himself is doing; and he will show him greater works than these, so that you will be astonished. Indeed, just as the Father raises the dead and gives them life, so also the Son gives life to whomever he wishes (5:20, 21).

This statement gives readers of the Fourth Gospel a glimpse of things to come. Jesus' words here anticipate the raising of Lazarus, the seventh sign. Jesus' words affirmed the convictions of the Jews: only God "worked" on the Sabbath. In the Fourth Gospel, we find Jesus also "working" on the Sabbath—works of restoration and new creation— because what God accomplished, Jesus accomplished. If the Jewish observers were amazed at pool healings on the Sabbath, just wait! Only God raised people from the dead. In the Fourth Gospel, Jesus raised someone from the dead, because what God accomplished, Jesus accomplished.

In the discourse that follows—laden as it is with theological significance—the narrative takes a fascinating turn. The accused— Jesus—takes on the role of accuser, while the accusers—the religious leaders—become the accused. Jesus cautions them: if one witnesses God working through the Son giving life to people and one does not honour the One who gives life, refusing to believe in him, that person will be judged. Instead of Jesus being on trial for breaking the Sabbath and for blasphemy, the Fourth Gospel has the reader understand it is the Jewish authorities who are really on trial (see John 5:19–29).

> Jesus' words affirmed the convictions of the Jews: only God "worked" on the Sabbath.

An open-ended story

As we read about Jesus and the Jews debating these controversial issues, what happened to the crippled man Jesus healed? The absence of any detail has not deterred speculation. Indeed, there is quite a bit of speculation concerning this character in the Fourth Gospel. He was not the typical character helped by Jesus who then associated himself with Jesus. Some wonder if the story is hinting that the man actually aligned himself with Jesus' enemies. At the very least, the man was not sure about his relationship to his healer.

As we have suggested, the Fourth Gospel probably reflects conversations taking place within the Christian community during the author's lifetime. Might this healed cripple reflect people in the community whose lives had been changed by Jesus, but whose loyalty was lacking for the long haul? How might this particular story—recorded only in the Fourth Gospel—have encouraged such individuals?

The Fourth Gospel introduces the crippled man with descriptions that kept readers wondering. After all, the man never said he wished to be healed. At first, the man did not know who had healed him, meaning he did not know Jesus' identity (5:13). When confronted by the Jews about carrying his bed mat on the Sabbath, the man pushed the blame on the one who had healed him (5:11). Throughout the story, the man is never described as "believing," a concept so crucial to this gospel. Nor is the man described as "following," which is what disciples do in this gospel.

Avoiding a clear resolution, this gospel leaves this man's story open-ended. When Jesus saw the man again in the temple, the man—by this time having learned Jesus' name—"thanked" his healer by turning Jesus in to the Jewish authorities (5:15). Is it possible that a man healed by Jesus became his enemy? Was the man one who sought to follow Jesus (1:38) or did he too become one who sought to kill him (5:18)? Is there another possible category? Is the man representing those who were just not sure about much of anything? He did not understand his healing, his religious leaders, his new role in society, or the expectations of his family and his faith community. After all, he had been in a place of the dying for 38 long years. That was almost the same length of time as Israel's barren wilderness experience—and readers familiar with the stories of the Pentateuch may well have made the connection. Was the healed man's wilderness experience over or not? Did he want to leave "the wilderness" or was he just too accustomed and conditioned to life beside the stagnant pool?

If we were to recap and reduce this encounter to its essence, the crippled man's first conversation with Jesus might sound something like this:

Jesus: "Do you want to be well?"
Man: "I can't get to the water."
Jesus: "The water of life has come to you."
Man: "Someone else always gets there first."

Jesus: "The living water is not for the fastest, it is for all."

Man: "No-one helps me."

Jesus: "The living water himself is offering to help you."

Man: "I'm so confused."

Jesus: "Stand up, take your mat and walk."

The healed man's conversation with the Jewish authorities went something like this:

Authorities: "Stop carrying your mat, it's the Sabbath!"

Man: "The man who healed me said to carry my mat."

Authorities: "Who healed you?"

Man: "I don't know."

The healed man did not know Jesus' identity and the narrative hints that he might not really want to know it. The man reminds me of one of my students many years ago. She came four minutes late to class almost every day of the school term. She did not seem to care that it would affect her grade. When she walked in, every bit of body language suggested that religion class was the last place she wanted to be. She had a collection of T-shirts that she wore that included statements on the front. One said, "I'm grumpy." Another warned, "Stay back, I'm angry." One was: "Bad attitude." I had to keep my chuckle to myself the day she walked in late, turned around and I read, "I'm a princess." Unfortunately there was no change in attitude that day.

> The healed man did not know Jesus' identity and the narrative hints that he might not really want to know it.

This young woman was so angry, and I was never able to learn why. She was suspended for several days for making some poor choices. When she returned, she was angrier than ever. Every day in class we read scenes from the gospels. Every day she refused to engage with the material. I wish that I could say that, by the end of the school term, she accepted Jesus into her life. I prayed that would happen. I found myself thinking about her as I prepared for classes, trying all kinds of approaches to reach her. But she indicated that she was not yet sure she wanted to know Jesus.

The sign of the Sabbath

The third sign in this gospel concerned a man who was healed beside a pool called Bethesda. And after Jesus healed him, Jesus found the man again. Jesus went to a place where it was risky for him, but Jesus went there anyway in order to find him. Jesus finds people again and again. Like a lost sheep, the one who was physically healed but still lost was found by Jesus again. In this second encounter, Jesus told him not to sin so something worse would not happen to him (5:14).

What could be worse than lying by a pool among the sick and dying for 38 years? The Fourth Gospel suggests that not knowing the identity of Jesus is worse. Far worse than a past of illness is a future without God. And this is why this miracle must take place on the Sabbath. The Sabbath itself is part of the sign!

The experience of the Sabbath is the experience of the presence of God. The Sabbath is the sign of God working to restore people. The Sabbath is the sign of God working to bring the living water to those "dried out" by life without God. The Sabbath is about experiencing the presence of God by pools and wells, in wilderness experiences and in temples. Sabbath is experiencing the presence of God, an experience that results in the healing of body and soul. The Sabbath is a gift offered to all, even to those who reject the healer, even to those who turn Jesus in to the authorities, getting him killed. The Sabbath is a sign of the presence of God given even to those who experience the miracle but miss the sign, to those who think the Sabbath is about carrying or not carrying mats.

This healing story that took place during the Sabbath hours serves the purpose of leading the reader to a richer understanding of Jesus' identity. Jesus was the Creator, working on the Sabbath to restore life. He was working to heal the whole world of sin's consequences. God was working to rid the world of cancer, AIDS, anorexia, arthritis, hunger, homelessness, abuse. The Sabbath was a sign that God restores humanity.

On the Sabbath at the pool, Jesus was not only healing, he was acting in ways that highlighted salvation. Like the other stories we have explored, this story anticipates the end of the Fourth Gospel. Then Jesus was not surrounded by the sick and dying at Bethesda but by the sick and dying at Golgotha, the ultimate place of "mercy" and "flowing water." The men on either side of Jesus did not have crippled or paralysed legs but their legs were broken in order to speed up the dying process (19:32). Jesus was not near a pool where the water occasionally flowed but at a cross where water flows out from Jesus' side (19:34).

It was not yet the Sabbath but it was getting close. And the religious leadership was more concerned with getting bodies off the crosses before Sabbath, than the welfare of the bodies themselves (19:31). They still noticed the mats, rather than the miracle. Would John's readers at least see the sign of the cross? Would they understand the sign of the Sabbath? Would they come to see more clearly that, through both the cross and the Sabbath, God was working to restore humanity?

On that Sabbath in Bethesda, Jesus would not stop working, for his Father was working. But the Sabbath following his crucifixion would be a day of rest for Jesus. The Sabbath, too, at its core was a sign of Jesus' true identity. The Sabbath was a sign of healing and restoration. The Sabbath was a sign of rest from the completed work of salvation: "It is finished" (19:30).

> Would they come to see more clearly that, through both the cross and the Sabbath, God was working to restore humanity?

May God forgive those of us who, as Sabbath keepers, have focused on mats instead of the miracle of healed men and women. Each week, as we welcome the Sabbath, may we understand it as a sign of wondrous truths about Jesus, salvation, healing and hope.

---

1. See Raymond E Brown's discussion in *The Gospel According to John I-XII*, The Anchor Bible series, Garden City, NY: Doubleday & Company, Inc, 1966, pages 206–7.

2. Notice that verse 4, included in many versions and in the NRSV as a footnote, probably reflected popular traditions surrounding the pool of Bethesda.

3. For a helpful discussion of proper interactions between women and men in the time of Jesus, see Bruce Malina, *The New Testament World: Insights from Cultural Anthropology* (revised edition), Louisville, KY: Westminster/John Knox Press, 1993.

4. Much has been written concerning the Fourth Gospel's use of the phrase "the Jews." Most scholars suggest that this phrase refers to a group of leaders among the Jewish community, probably located in Jerusalem. For an interesting contemporary reflection on the Fourth Gospel by a Jewish woman, see Adele Reinhartz, *Befriending the Beloved Disciple: A Jewish Reading of the Gospel of John*, New York: Continuum, 2001.

Chapter 5

Signs of Liberation

John 6:1–71

Two of the Fourth Gospel's seven carefully narrated signs are found in John 6. For these fourth and fifth signs, Jesus was back in his home territory of Galilee. As John introduces this new episode, he explains that it is some time after Jesus returned from his second visit to Jerusalem and Jesus had located his ministry near the Sea of Galilee.

John gives readers a hint into the issues surrounding the two signs explored in this chapter: "A large crowd kept following him, because they saw the signs that he was doing for the sick" (6:2). Only two of the signs John has told us about concern healing sick people but it seems the crowds are responding to numerous healings. This comment reminds us that John has carefully selected the stories he wants to tell in his gospel. Undoubtedly each of the other occasions of healing had their own central character and story. John has a theological purpose in choosing the stories he wants to share (John 20:30, 31). And once again, we remember the categories of characters and their responses in the Fourth Gospel: those who refused to believe in the signs; those who focused on the signs, rather than the insight into Jesus' identity that the signs pointed to; those who, through the signs, came to believe in Jesus; and those who believe in Jesus even before witnessing a sign.

Given the way the large crowd is described in verse 2, it would seem they fell into the second category. They followed Jesus and in that sense they were his disciples (6:5). But they were more focused superficially on the signs Jesus did, than on the real character and identity of the One they were following. Now they witnessed not healing miracles but signs that would remind them of their ancestors' experience of the Exodus—that moment of national beginning, when as God's people they were liberated from forced slavery in the land of Egypt. The two signs concern the miraculous provision of food—bread from heaven, as it were—and a miracle of making the sea behave on command. It seems that they interpreted the signs from a purely materialistic and political perspective and figured that with this kind of ability, Jesus surely could gain them independence from the hated Roman occupation. They wanted to make Jesus their king. But the Fourth Gospel presents Jesus as a Messiah whose signs point to a cross. While Jesus will transform the agony of crucifixion into an event that glorifies God, the crowd interprets the signs as pointing to an earthly Messiah, a Moses-like leader.

Near the Passover

In addition to locating Jesus near the Sea of Galilee (6:1), the Fourth Gospel gives another location marker as it described this scene. The author connects the whole story to Passover: "Now the Passover, the festival of the Jews, was near" (6:4). It would seem this is not an incidental marker of time. Rather it is establishing a meaning marker. It was getting close to Passover, that high day of all high days! For the Jews, it was the greatest festival of all. It was the celebration you did your best to witness first-hand by going to Jerusalem.

It was also the festival that the Romans feared the most because civic affairs became so chaotic and hard to manage. Because it was a time when Jews were thinking about their ancestors' freedom from Egypt and rehearsing the key events of the grand story, political tensions ran high and aspirations soared. Rome did not like Jewish subjects contemplating freedom. Palestine had to be controlled tightly. It was a strategic and military necessity. How could they keep the wild Parthians to the east of the Jewish territories at bay unless they controlled the Jews with an iron grip?[1] So the air was filled with tension and anticipation.

Jewish zealots—the radical right wing of Jewish politics—often took advantage of the Passover festival to encourage rebellion against the

Roman overlords. Pilate—the Roman governor of Jerusalem—always had soldiers in reserve at this time of the year, standing by in case any trouble boiled over. Even more soldiers than usual stood guard in marketplaces and they maintained a visible presence around the temple area. The Jewish priests (Sadducees) did their best to maintain order, especially in the temple courtyards, to ensure that soldiers need not be called in, defiling the holy places with their Gentile feet.

Every Jewish family prepared carefully for Passover. Whether young or old, all participated in the ceremonial meal and reflected on its meaning, including the splashed blood on doorposts. They recounted the story about leaving the land of captivity and crossing through the Red Sea, the manna God sent from the sky, and the water that came from the rock.

After the Fourth Gospel primed readers' imaginations by this strategic mention of Passover, it described Jesus sitting down near the Sea of Galilee and noticing that the people were hungry. The crowd was described as "large" (6:5), numbering 5000 (6:10), possibly pilgrims on the way to Jerusalem for the festival. With so many people present, the scene depicted a major food shortage. Although it was a time of festivity, these people did not have any bread. It was Passover time, but the crowd was starving for so many things—for food and security, for freedom and hope.

New manna?

Addressing their immediate need for food, Jesus took five barley loaves. Cheaper than wheat, barley was the food of the poor. Jesus took the barley loaves and two dried fish, and fed thousands of people "as much as they wanted" (6:11). Anthropologists who study first-century Palestine tell us that the vast majority of people barely survived day to day, year to year. In Jesus' day, it was probably rare to eat as much as one wanted, getting the minimum of what one needed to survive was struggle enough.

Back in their hometown synagogues, when the people heard the scroll of Exodus read, they heard the story of bread coming down from heaven to sustain their ancestors and to keep them from starvation. The food came after experiencing freedom from Egypt. As long as their ancestors lived in the wilderness, they "gathered as much [food] as each of them needed" (Exodus 16:18). As Jesus multiplied food and the members in the multitude each ate as much as they wanted, the people must have wondered, *Was it happening again? Was bread coming down from heaven again? What was this that they were experiencing by the shores of the Sea of Galilee? Was another "Passover" about to occur? Was freedom from Rome right around the corner? What did this amazing miracle mean? What event did this sign point to?*

Many people of the first century believed that in the last days—at the final time of freedom from foreign rulers—God would provide manna again. A Midrash on Exodus 16:25 read: "You will not find it [manna] in this age, but you shall find it in the age that is coming."[2] A Midrash on Ecclesiastes 1:9 read: "As the first redeemer caused manna to descend . . . so will the latter redeemer cause manna to descend."[3] After Jesus multiplied the food, the Fourth Gospel says: "When the people saw the sign that he had done, they began to say, 'This is indeed the prophet who is to come into the world'" (6:14). They saw a revolt in the making, with manna provided in abundance.

But Jesus knew they were looking at the sign without seeing that the sign pointed to him in unique and unexpected ways. They liked signs—and they liked speculating on what might happen in the near future, as God broke into history and put Rome in its proper place. The crowd wanted a king who could make bread. But the "bread of life" Jesus spoke of was not what they had in mind. This was bread and life that would shape a new kind of kingdom. So Jesus left them and went off by himself into the hills (6:15).

A new exodus

The crowds camped along the beaches, but the smaller group of close disciples started rowing into the night across the sea back to Capernaum. And Jesus joined them! After the children of Israel ate their original Passover meal, they left Egypt by crossing the parted Red Sea, walking on dry land. Here in this story the Creator of the land and sea, bread and fish, crossed over on top of the water! The Creator caused the rough winds to stop blowing and the waves to stop beating against the boat.

There are more significant links with the Exodus story. In the book of Exodus, Moses asked the voice coming out of the burning bush, "When people ask who sent me, whom shall I say?" And God responded: "'I AM'! sent you . . ." (Exodus 3:14). The Fourth Gospel declared: "When [the disciples] had rowed about three or four miles, they saw Jesus walking on the sea and coming near the boat, and they were terrified. But [Jesus] said to them: "I AM—do not be afraid" (6:19, 20). Although most English versions have something like, "It is I," the Greek words are exactly the same as elsewhere in this gospel, *ego eimi*—"I AM"—and the careful reader would have noted it immediately.[4] Jesus was performing the miracles of the Exodus!

The acts of divinity that brought liberation to Israel at the first Passover were being remembered through the actions of Jesus by the Sea of Galilee at Passover season. A new exodus was taking place! It was a new kind of homecoming. A new kingdom was being established. God had brought their ancestors out of Egypt to a promised land and now God was once again giving them bread from heaven and controlling the sea. The "I AM" had said, "Do not be afraid."

"The Crisis in Galilee"

Many people in our world today are afraid, and fear sometimes causes us to do terrible things to each other. I was living in Washington, DC, when the hijacked planes went into the twin towers in New York City, and into the Pentagon in Northern Virginia. In a matter of minutes, I heard fighter jets above my head, protecting the part of the Eastern Seaboard in which I was living. The radio and TV were non-stop in their coverage of this "attack of war." For many days to come, people were in a state of panic. Fear motivated choices made by individuals, local communities and civic institutions. This very human emotion can cloud our judgment, even as it narrows our focus and consumes our energies.

John 6 tells of a crisis at sea, a life-and-death struggle. And then Jesus walked across the raging water and said, "I AM—do not be afraid."

The first readers of the Fourth Gospel were quite probably women and men who had little to feel secure about. They were part of the Roman Empire, yet they served a different king and kingdom. They had Jewish roots theologically, socially and culturally, but they were no longer welcomed in the synagogues.[5] So they formed Christian house churches—small companies of people, probably no more than 30 people, the maximum possible in the largest homes of the day. They were small groups of Christian believers at odds with much of the society around them. They related well to a story of disciples caught in a storm on the sea. Fishing boats in Jesus' day held few people. And the boats of the day did not provide much shelter from raging storms. But "I AM!" said Jesus. "Do not be afraid."

In this story of the disciples on the sea, readers may be tempted to see the buffeted boat in the storm as the crisis. In many Bibles, this section of the gospel record is identified as "The Crisis in Galilee." But the real crisis was not a stormy sea, nor even the Roman occupation. The real crisis centred on the identity of Jesus, the "I AM," and the decision each disciple must make. The great multitude eventually found Jesus back on the other side of the sea near Capernaum again. It is then that they asked a question that sets up the lengthy discourse that comprises the rest of this chapter: "When did you come here?"

They are startled because they did not see Jesus get into a boat. Yet the writer, John, used their question to focus the reader on Jesus' identity. "When did you come here?" Perhaps readers remembered the words at the start of this gospel: "The Word became flesh and lived among us" (1:14). The question lingers on in the mind of the reader. "When did you come here?" Seven times in this chapter alone, Jesus said: "I have come down from heaven" (6:33, 38, 41, 42, 50, 51, 58).

Food that endures

Jesus challenged the intentions of this great multitude:

> Jesus answered them, "Very truly, I tell you, you are looking for me, not because you saw signs, but because you ate your fill of the loaves. Do not work for the food that perishes, but for the food that endures for eternal life, which the Son of Man will give you" (6:26, 27).

Yesterday their hunger was satisfied, but today the crowd was hungry again. They were ready for breakfast. In one of her books on the Fourth Gospel, Gail O'Day sees the crowd as reflecting the human "appetite for consumption."[6] No amount was ever enough, because they focused on the sign instead of the reality to which it pointed. But Jesus invited the crowd to "work for the food that endures for eternal life" (6:27). Such food was the "work of God." It was to believe in the One God had sent (6:29).

And then the crowd asks a question that must have caused John's first readers to cringe: "What sign are you going to give us then, so that we may see it and believe you? What work are you performing? Our ancestors ate the manna in the wilderness" (6:30, 31). They continued by saying that Moses had given their ancestors bread to eat, and their reply seems to infer that they considered the giving of the manna to be more amazing than yesterday's miraculous meal. After all, the manna came down *every day* for 40 years. What sign are you going to do, Jesus? And Jesus replied: "Very truly, I tell you, it was not Moses who gave you the bread from heaven, but it is my Father who gives you the true bread from heaven. For the bread of God is that which comes down from heaven and gives life to the world" (6:32, 33).

And then the crowd asks a question that must have caused John's first readers to cringe.

Jesus said they had several things very wrong. First, their ancestors received bread from God, not from Moses. Yahweh was the source of the miraculous manna. Second, the description of bread was about the present, not the past. Third, the manna did not endure; it was not able to keep. But the bread provided by Jesus remained! The disciples had gathered the leftovers (6:12, 13), illustrating bread that did not perish but could be shared with others. Fourth, the manna was not only for their ancestors, but the true bread from heaven was given by God to the whole world (3:16)!

In the last book of the New Testament, this multitude of 5000 people becomes a great multitude that no-one can count, made up of men, women and children from every nation, tribe, language and people (see Revelation 7:9–17). The crowd sounded like the Samaritan woman in Chapter 4 when they responded: "Sir, give us this bread always" (6:34, compare 4:15).

Now Jesus had their attention and he explained how these signs pointed to him: "I am . . . the bread of life. Whoever comes to me will never be hungry" (6:35). And later, "Anyone who comes to me I will never drive away" (6:37). The hopes of Passover extended even into eternity: "All who see the Son and believe in him may have eternal life and I will raise them up on the last day" (6:40).

The Fourth Gospel clearly enjoys using directional language as a way to underscore spiritual realities: Jesus—the bread from heaven—came down; those who ate the bread will rise up. Their ancestors, who ate manna, still died. But if one eats the bread of life, one experiences eternal life. The crowd said: What is this guy talking about? He's Joseph's son (6:42).

At this point in the narrative, the Fourth Gospel calls the crowd "Judeans," probably not because they are from Judea, for earlier these people seemed to be from the region of the Galilee (6:1, 2). But to the author of this gospel, "Judeans" were those who said "no" to Jesus, those who refused to believe. They dismissed Jesus as "Joseph's son." But careful readers knew this statement was inadequate. Those who had followed the Fourth Gospel from its beginning knew Jesus' origins were not with Joseph and Mary, but with God: "In the beginning was the Word and the Word was with God, and the Word was God" (1:1). The crisis point had arrived. Decisions must be made. Will this crowd of disciples see through the signs to the true identity of Jesus?

The Bread of Life

Giving further insights into his identity, Jesus said: "Those who eat my flesh and drink my blood abide in me, and I in them. . . . This is the bread that came down from heaven, not like that which your ancestors ate, and they died. But the one who eats this bread will live forever" (6:56, 58). It is important to note that for the author of the Fourth Gospel, the Passover meal became the celebration of the Eucharist.[7] But the crowd responds: No! No! "This teaching is difficult; who can accept it?" (6:60). And the narrator states: "Because of this many of his disciples turned back and no longer went about with him" (6:66). They wanted signs—but not signs like this.

One of Jesus' most human moments in John's gospel followed this exchange. As the crowd left, Jesus asked the 12 disciples, "'Do you also wish to go away?' Simon Peter answered him, 'Lord, to whom can we go? You have the words of eternal life. We have come to believe and know that you are the Holy One of God'" (6:67–69).

Most of the members of the multitude—those who had eaten the miraculous bread and fish—left Jesus. But some remained. Some believed that Jesus was the Holy One of God. For John's community of believers—the original readers of the Fourth Gospel—the language of eating bread and drinking wine had become the language of the Eucharist, the celebration of the Lord's Supper. Those who embraced this gospel remembered that Jesus received the food from the little boy. Then Jesus thanked God. And then Jesus distributed the bread. This was what disciples of Jesus were called to do with the bread of life: to receive it, to thank God for it, then to distribute it to others.

Careful readers will notice that there are two different ways of understanding the Passover at the end of the Fourth Gospel. In one, the Jewish authorities, who were trying to get Jesus condemned to death, refused to enter into Pilate's headquarters, so they would not defile themselves (18:28). If they were defiled, they would not be able to properly observe the Passover celebration. On Passover preparation day, they wanted to stay clean so they could say the prayers and perform the sacrifices. They needed to be clean in order to pour out the blood, to eat the Passover bread and to celebrate the liberation of their ancestors from Egypt at the hand of the great "I AM."

In the other Passover celebration, the "Lamb that takes away the sins of the world" (1:29) stood in Pilate's headquarters. On Passover preparation day, having already washed the feet of his disciples (13:1–20) and having already prayed for them (17:1–26), he was sacrificed. Jesus' blood was poured out, his body broken. His sacrifice made possible the liberation of all people from slavery to sin (3:16). The crucified one—the great "I AM"—proclaimed, "It is finished" (19:30). Because of this act by the great "I AM," no-one need be afraid.

If you have ever experienced a gathering of people from dozens of countries, with native dress and music, you know the excitement of such an experience. The book of Revelation describes such a scene, with an uncountable great multitude standing before the Lamb. The signs of liberation are included—the marriage supper of the Lamb, where there is plenty for all, and the sea of glass that never gets chaotic and stormy, a sea that everyone can walk over (see Revelation 19:9; 15:2).

These signs declare that bondage is finally over. It will be the ultimate homecoming. There will be no more slavery, exile, disease or death. And the great multitude will proclaim with Peter: "You have the words of eternal life. We have come to believe and know that you are the Holy One of God" (6:68, 69).

1. The Parthian Empire, located on the eastern border of the Roman Empire, regularly threatened Rome's eastern territories.

2. While "Midrash" can refer to a book of teachings, here it is meant as an interpretation of a particular verse of Scripture.

3. Raymond E Brown states: "We have evidence in later Jewish documents of a popular expectation that in the final days God would again provide manna—an expectation connected with the hopes of a second Exodus." Brown then mentions Midrash Mekilta on Exodus 16:25, and Midrash Rabbah on Ecclesiastes 1:9. See Brown, *The Gospel According to John I-XII*, The Anchor Bible Commentary 29, Garden City, NY: Doubleday & Company, Inc, 1966, page 265.

4. This was a formulaic expression alluding to Jesus' divinity that John wanted his readers to notice.

5. Although debated, there are scholars who still accept some version of the theory proposed by J Louis Martyn in *History and Theology in the Fourth Gospel* (3rd edition), Louisville, KY: Westminster John Knox Press, 2003, that the text, especially John 9, reflects some type of conflict between Jews and Jewish Christians.

6. Gail R O'Day, *The Word Disclosed: Preaching the Gospel of John* (revised edition), St Louis, MO: Chalice Press, 2002, page 121.

7. The reference to Judas at the end of this chapter (6:70, 71) further supports the idea that this scene is John's Eucharist scene. I am grateful to John Brunt for bringing this reference to Judas to my attention.

Chapter 6

Sign of God's Work

John 9:1–41

According to the Fourth Gospel, the third time Jesus journeyed up to Jerusalem he went particularly to participate in the Festival of Booths—also called *Sukkot* or the "Feast of Tabernacles." The Feast of Tabernacles usually took place some time between late September and late October, depending on the year. It followed just five days after the most solemn of all ritual Jewish festivals—the *Yom Kippur*—and it was celebrated in bright contrast to the sombre Day of Atonement.

Sukkot was the most joyous of the festivals because it doubled as a harvest celebration. It was intended to help Israel recall the events of its wilderness wanderings. On the first night of the festival as it was celebrated in Jerusalem in Jesus' day, the candle-lighting ceremony took place in the brightly illuminated Court of Women, where four large candlesticks were lit and the elders celebrated a candle dance. Later Jesus challenged his hearers with the claim: "I am the light of the world. Whoever follows me will never walk in darkness but will have the light of life" (8:12). On the last day of the festival, in a ceremony of song and dance, the water-pouring ritual took place. It was an Israelite version of a prayer for rain for the crops during the coming year. Israel sought God's blessing on the rain that they might not be thirsty.

The water-pouring ceremony began with a choir brightly chanting the words of Isaiah 12:3: "With joy you will draw water from the wells of salvation." They sang the words of the ancient prophet as the priest filled a golden pitcher with water from the pool of Siloam. Then with music and dancing, they proceded up to the temple through the Water Gate. At the entrance to the temple, the priest poured the water on the altar of sacrifice.

At some point during these celebrations, Jesus interrupted things. From the way the author of the Fourth Gospel narrates his story, it seems that right in this context Jesus cried out, "Let anyone who is thirsty come to me, and let the one who believes in me drink. As the scripture has said, 'Out of the believer's heart shall flow rivers of living water'" (7:37b, 38).[1]

The interruption of the formal program of festivities disturbed many people. After this festival, the One who "became flesh and did tabernacle among us"[2] was almost killed when other people attending the ceremonies picked up stones to throw at Jesus (8:59). But Jesus was nimble enough to "slip away" and escape from the temple grounds. This was high drama.

But the next verse links us with the important story that follows: "As [Jesus] walked along, he saw a man blind from birth" (9:1). Jesus met a man born blind. Jesus' sixth sign in this gospel concerns the healing of this man. This man's story was one that also involved water and was certainly about light. And John wants us to notice both.

More than debate

As Jesus and his disciples walked by the man born blind, the disciples asked Jesus: "Rabbi, who sinned, this man or his parents, that he was born blind?" (9:2). In this time and place, people assumed illness was an indication of God's disfavour due to the sinful behaviour of the deformed or diseased. But a theological debate of the day had centred on the phenomenon of newborns with physical problems. Had such a baby sinned in the womb? How could that be?

Jesus' response to this "heavy" question was simply to dismiss the debate. Jesus told his disciples that a suffering person was not an occasion for a debate on why there was suffering in the world. For Jesus and for Jesus' followers, a suffering person constituted a call to do God's work, which was to alleviate suffering (9:3, 4). Jesus said, "Neither this man nor his parents sinned; he was born blind so that God's works might be revealed in him.[3] We must work the works of him who sent me while it is day; night is coming when no-one can work. As long as I am in the world, I am the light of the world" (9:3–5). The earlier reference to the Feast of Tabernacles and memories of candle-lighting ceremonies underscored Jesus' words. If the blind man was an occasion for a debate, and not a call to act, who was really in the dark? Who was blind to the true identity of Jesus?

Recently I had an exceptional group of students taking a course on the gospels. One of their major assignments involved spending four hours serving people who embodied the kinds of people Jesus served throughout Luke's gospel. They could choose from a variety of service opportunities, including proposing one of their own if they wished. Some chose to work at shelters set up for the victims of the then-recent southern California fires. Some worked in soup kitchens, others volunteered to work with children in after-school programs.

One young man in the class became frustrated with his service learning arrangements because everything he proposed fell through. A food drive at his church was cancelled. Then a trip into Mexico to volunteer at a clinic was re-scheduled for after the school term. Nothing seemed to work out.

If the blind man was an occasion for a debate, and not a call to act, who was really in the dark?

So one day he drove into Los Angeles to help out at a soup kitchen. He could not believe it when he arrived to find that the soup kitchen had unexpectedly closed for the rest of the morning. My student told me he was sitting in his car trying to calm himself by praying. That was when a six- or seven-year-old boy started washing his front windshield.

The student got out of the car and started talking to the boy. He noticed the boy's worn clothes and holes in his shoes. He asked how he might help the boy and immediately the boy said, "We need food! My mum works hard all day—and we are so hungry."

The student went with the boy to the grocery store and bought various food items, then took the food to the boy's apartment. He was shocked to find three other children there—all younger than his new friend—

alone in the house. While their mother worked, it was the oldest child's job to make some extra money washing car windows. Although this was a regular school day, the boy was needed to bring in whatever coins he could to help fund the family's food and rent expenses. My student told me later in his reflection report that he could not help himself. He knew that the Jesus of the gospels would do more to help this family. So he went and purchased clothes for the children. The oldest boy kept saying over and over again how happy their mother would be when she came home late that night.

Who sinned—this boy or his mother—that he should be born so poor and so hungry? If the suffering one simply becomes an occasion for a debate, rather than a call to act, who is in the dark? Who is really blind?

The miracle

After Jesus said he was the "light of the world," this story continues by discussing spit and mud: "He spat on the ground and made mud with the saliva and spread the mud on the man's eyes, saying to him, 'Go, wash in the pool of Siloam' (which means 'the one who has been sent'). Then he went" (9:6, 7a). This part of the description, which my students often consider quite disgusting, was probably not an unusual act by miracle-workers in Jesus' day. The saliva of miracle-workers was believed to have medicinal value and such a mixture may have been used for people with an eye injury. What was amazing about this scene was that even the best miracle-worker would not even attempt to cure a person blind since birth. Jesus treated this man as a man able to be cured. And the man did exactly as he was told. Like the royal official, he took Jesus at his word.

Some scholars who reflect on this scene consider it a re-enactment of God's creation of humanity. In the beginning at Creation (see Genesis 1:1; 2:7), there was dust—and God created out of the dust. In this new beginning (John 1:1; 9:6), there was dust and spit (water)—and Jesus re-created out of the dust. There was no conversation except to "Go wash in a pool."[4] The unusual name of the pool means "the one who has been sent."

Careful readers of this gospel see the connection. They know that Jesus is the One Sent by God (7:29). So a pool called "the one who has been sent" was a metaphor for Jesus. He was the source of water for the water-pouring ceremony (7:37, 38). Jesus was the source of water for the blind man's healing—and Jesus was also the source of light. The narrative does not make its readers wait long to find out what happened: "He went and washed and came back able to see" (9:7).

It is easy to pass quickly over verse 7, especially if we have heard this story many times before. Finding his way to Siloam in the dark, the man doubtless needed his stick and some friends to show him the way. But he came home able to see! A blind man, who had never seen before, could see. I wonder what conversation Jesus and the man had the first time he could look into Jesus' eyes. I wonder what things around him the man noticed for the first time.

I remember well the day I got glasses. As a fourth-grader, I could not believe how many things I had been missing. With my new glasses, it was almost impossible to focus on one thing, because my eyes kept jumping, noticing detail after detail. That was the experience of getting glasses for a near-sighted, seeing person. Just imagine what this man was experiencing with his new sight. And soon he finds himself the object of much village conversation.

The reaction

The neighbours start arguing: Is this the fellow who used to beg around here? Some said, "No, it can't be, just looks like him" (9:8, 9). Many of the people who had walked by the blind beggar had never really seen him. Scripture says that the man himself kept saying, "I am the man" (9:9b). But they kept asking him, "Then how were your eyes opened?" (9:10). So he told them what Jesus did (9:11).

Even before there was time for a party, a proper celebration, the story turns dark. The readers are told: "They brought to the Pharisees the man who had formerly been blind." The gospel explains ominously, "Now it was a Sabbath day when Jesus made the mud and opened his eyes" (9:13, 14). Jesus was in trouble again.

R Alan Culpepper has noticed 11 similarities between this story and the man at the pool of Bethesda.[5] Of course, both miracles took place near pools—one at Bethesda and the other at Siloam. In both stories of healing, Jesus took the initiative. But a key point John wants us to notice is that in both stories Jesus is accused of violating the Sabbath.

As we might have guessed when we read verse 14, the debate about a suffering person shifted into a debate about Sabbath-keeping. Was Jesus really a miracle-worker or one who broke the holy Sabbath? More importantly, was Jesus from God—or not? After interrogating the man born blind, the Pharisees were ready to believe he had never really been blind. So they brought in his parents for interrogation:

> "Is this your son, who you say was born blind? How then does he now see?" His parents answered, "We know that this is our son, and that he was born blind; but we do not know how it is that now he sees, nor do we know who opened his eyes. Ask him; he is of age. He will speak for himself" (9:19–21).

In order for their son to be "of age," he had to be at least 13 years old. Just how much older he was, is not clear. Whatever his age, this day should have been a day of great joy for him and for his parents. Their son could see! He once was blind, but now he could see. Their son's whole life had been in darkness, his only possible future that of a beggar. But now he could see.

This was the first time he had ever seen his parents. Yet, as the three looked at each other in wonder, the parents were placed in a position of standing with their son or with the only community they had ever known. What should have been a day of great joy—a day both parents and son had longed for—had become a day of danger. The story continues:

> His parents said this because they were afraid of the Jews; for the Jews had already agreed that anyone who confessed Jesus to be the Messiah would be put out of the synagogue. Therefore his parents said, "He is of age; ask him" (9:22, 23).

The author of the Fourth Gospel is not only telling the story of Jesus in Jerusalem, he is reflecting the reality of his day. Perhaps as he writes, Jewish Christians in major cities all over Asia Minor were being expelled from the synagogues.

Some contemporary readers of the Fourth Gospel know what it is like to be forced to make this heart-wrenching choice between family and faith. Does one side with one's religion or one's relatives? Do you stand with your son or your synagogue? Probably many among John's first readers knew what it was like to leave family when they were forced out of the synagogue for proclaiming Jesus as the Christ. Those forcing the blind man's parents with this horrendous decision refused to let up: "So for the second time they called the man who had been blind, and they said to him, 'Give glory to God! We know that this man is a sinner.' He answered, 'I do not know whether he is a sinner. One thing I do know, that though I was blind, now I see'" (9:24, 25).

Giving their testimonies

The man testified to what he was sure about—his own personal experience. The healed blind man was not like the man healed at Bethesda's pool (5:1–18). Rather than turn Jesus in, this healed man witnessed to what Jesus did in his life. This man had not known about Jesus for long. He did not finish college, nor did he have the privilege of attending a seminary or earning a doctorate in New Testament studies. Yet he preached a powerful sermon to the first-century scholars: "One thing I do know, that though I was blind, now I see" (9:25).

Not all of us are preacher-types. Some of us get knots in our stomachs just thinking about standing up in front of a crowd. But each can share in our own unique way the one thing we know—our own stories. Sadly, the man's interrogators rejected his testimony and we hear the deep irony:[6]

> They said to him, "What did he do to you? How did he open your eyes?" He answered them, "I have told you already, and you would not listen. Why do you want to hear it again? Do you also want to become his disciples?" Then they reviled him, saying, "You are his disciple, but we are disciples of Moses. We *know* that God has spoken to Moses, but as for this man, *we do not know where he comes from*" (9:26-29, emphasis supplied).

As they said these words, they condemned themselves. They were ignorant of Jesus' origins. That was the difference between those who rejected Jesus or fixated on his signs, and those who accepted Jesus. In the end, the four groups actually reduce to two: those who walked away from Jesus, and those who said to him: "You are the Holy One of God."

The first group did not know where Jesus came from, but the second group knew his true origins.

All along we see this happening in the telling of the signs. We see just two groups emerging—those who know and those who do not. At the wedding in Cana, after Jesus performed his first sign, the steward tasted the wine, without knowing the source of the delicious drink. But those who had filled the water jars, who had done whatever Jesus told them to do, they knew the source of the miraculous wine.

At the healing miracle in Cana, after Jesus performed his second sign, the royal official's servants did not know why the fever taking the life of their master's little boy suddenly left. But the royal official knew where the healing power came from, that Jesus' words had healed his son.

At the pool in Bethesda, after Jesus performed his third sign, the healed man at the pool did not know Jesus' name; he did not know the name of his healer. But as the narrative unfolds, the reader comes to understand that Jesus and the Father are One, and that both were working to restore human life on the Sabbath.

Near the Sea of Galilee, after Jesus performed his fourth sign, the crowd did not realise that the bread of life was much more than a free meal on the sea shore. It meant accepting Jesus at a much deeper level, taking in the True Bread from heaven. The crowd abandoned Jesus (6:66). But the 12 disciples knew where Jesus came from and that he had the words of eternal life.

On the other side of Galilee, after Jesus performed his fifth sign, the crowd crossed the sea but did not understand where Jesus came from. But those in the boat knew that the "I AM" walks on water, even raging water. They did not need to fear.

At the pool of Siloam, after Jesus performed his sixth sign, those interrogating the man said about Jesus, "We don't know where he comes from." But the now-seeing man knew better. He knew that the One able to cure him was of God. The last thing the healed blind man said to the Pharisees was: "If this man were not from God, he could do nothing" (9:33).

The unpleasant experience of the man having to appear before the religious leaders caused him to see even more clearly. John's readers who were themselves undergoing persecution came through the experience with clearer understandings concerning Jesus' identity. Suffering was not an occasion for a debate. Rather it was a call to act faithfully and to see with new eyes. The focus of the story was not about gaining physical sight, as much as it was about the ability to see spiritually: to understand at a deeper level the truth about God and about Jesus.

Questions and responses

The Pharisees' last words to the healed blind man are: "You were born entirely in sins, and are you trying to teach us?" And this section closes with the words: "And they drove him out" (9:34). But even though he was expelled, and no longer able to be part of his faith community, he saw more clearly than ever before, both physically and spiritually. The Pharisees were so sure of what they knew. But in reality, their eyes were blind to the new things God would have them see. By denying the light of the world, they were plunged into darkness: "And this is the judgment, that the light has come into the world, and people loved darkness rather than light because their deeds were evil" (3:19).

> Even though he was expelled, and no longer able to be part of his faith community, he saw more clearly than ever before, both physically and spiritually.

Later in this gospel, when Jesus was brought to Pilate, Pilate considered the matter a religious issue. He thought the Jews should handle such religious disagreements according to their own laws (18:31), perhaps as they might deal with a blind man healed on the Sabbath. But, according to the Fourth Gospel, the Jewish leadership insisted on Pilate condemning Jesus to death. Pilate asked the question that those who missed the point of Jesus' signs cannot answer: "Where are you from?" (19:9).

Most were in the dark and could not see that he was from God. But, thankfully, "The light shines in the darkness, and the darkness did not overcome it" (1:5). While those "plunged into darkness" prepared to crucify him, Pilate asked, "Where are you from?" And in the course of their conversations, Jesus gives Pilate a number of answers: "My kingdom is not from this world" (18:36); "My kingdom is not from here" (18:36); "You would have no power over me unless it had been given you from above" (19:11).

The healed blind man's story does not end in expulsion from the synagogue. The Fourth Gospel continues:

> Jesus heard that they had driven out [the man born blind], and when he found him, he said, "Do you believe in the Son of Man?" He answered, "And who is he, sir? Tell me, so that I may believe in him." Jesus said to him, "You have seen him, and the one speaking with you is he." He said, "Lord I believe" and worshipped him (9:35–38).

Just as the Good Shepherd in the next chapter (see John 10:1–18) went out to find the lost sheep, here in this story Jesus went out to find the one who had been expelled from the synagogue. The man born blind gave glory to God through his testimony and through his worship. Yes, he was physically healed in an instant but his spiritual healing was gradual.

It is the same now. An individual is confronted by Jesus, begins to believe and follows his word, goes to the pool, gets baptised and joins a church. But the believer with a new kind of eyesight spends a lifetime learning insights into Jesus' identity. This story challenges contemporary church leaders to be patient with new believers rather than threatened by their questions. What new insights into Jesus can people whose eyes have been recently opened teach the rest of the community of faith?

A deeper experience with Jesus

The Fourth Gospel is a place to go for those longing to deepen an experience with God. Perhaps we had our eyes opened years ago but we are longing to grow in our faith. This gospel can lead us to that renewed encounter with Jesus.[7] I have seen it happen time and time again. Students begin a school term registering for "The Gospel of John" because it fits best into their schedule. Perhaps the course meets an elective requirement, seems like an easy "A" or is required for their program. But then they encounter the Jesus of this gospel.

Like Nicodemus, they have many difficult questions. But they find a Jesus willing to meet them at night—or whenever—and not condemn them for their questions. They encounter a Jesus who surprises them, much like he surprised the Samaritan woman at the well. They encounter a Jesus who begins a healing process long before they have grasped the meaning behind his question, "Do you want to be well?" As they encounter Jesus at weddings, pools, hillsides and on the lake, they come to see him in new ways.

Jerusalem had just celebrated the Feast of Tabernacles—and the Word "became flesh and did tabernacle among us" (1:14). Jerusalem had just experienced a water-pouring ceremony and the water Source called "the One who has been sent" had provided healing, living water. Jerusalem had just experienced a candle-lighting ceremony and the Light of the world had overcome darkness—physical darkness for the man born blind and spiritual darkness for all humanity. Jerusalem had just celebrated the Feast of Tabernacles and a healed beggar realised that the place to give glory to God was at the feet of Jesus. He said, "Lord, I believe."

In the Fourth Gospel, resurrection morning begins "while it was still dark" (20:1). Like the story of the man born blind, new life begins in darkness. And then "the light of the world" encounters people who are crippled, blind and mourning—and suddenly Jesus changes their lives forever.

1. For a helpful discussion of this festival, see R Alan Culpepper, *The Gospel and Letters of John*, Nashville, TN: Abingdon Press, 1998, pages 164–70.

2. John 1:14, *Young's Literal Translation*, Grand Rapids, MI: Baker Book House, 1898.

3. While Jesus' comment may sound more troubling to contemporary ears than the debate he challenges, Jesus is not giving an explanation for the presence of suffering in the world. Instead, John will equate the alleviation of the man's suffering with the very purpose of Jesus' ministry and God's work on earth.

4. Clearly, John wants his readers to understand that Jesus was sensitive to the social expectations and the context for this man being accepted back into his community. The stone pool was an accepted place for ritual cleansing and Jesus wanted the man to follow accepted custom. But there was also a deeper meaning, since this gospel has already referred to Jesus as the "living water."

5. R Alan Culpepper, *Anatomy of the Fourth Gospel: A Study in Literary Design*, Philadelphia, PA: Fortress Press, 1983, pages 139–40.

6. ibid, pages 165–80, discusses John's irony as two levels of understanding which are ultimately incompatible. Readers are challenged to adopt the "higher" meaning, joining the implied author in adequate comprehension.

7. One helpful work is the small book by Raymond E Brown, *A Retreat with John the Evangelist: That You May Have Life*, Cincinnati, OH: St Anthony Messenger Press, 1998.

Chapter 7

Sign of Glory

John 11:1–57

Our journey through the Fourth Gospel's seven signs has taken us twice to Cana in the Galilean hills, to the village of Sychar in Samaria, to a pool called Bethesda, to the grassy shoreline of the Sea of Galilee and then to another pool called Siloam in central Jerusalem. The location of the seventh and final sign finds us back in Judea at a small town on the eastern outskirts of Jerusalem on the slopes of Olivet.

The Fourth Gospel sets the scene of this seventh sign in a strange way:

> Now a certain man was ill, Lazarus of Bethany, the village of
> Mary and her sister Martha. Mary was the one who anointed
> the Lord with perfume and wiped his feet with her hair; her
> brother Lazarus was ill. So the sisters sent a message to Jesus,
> "Lord, he whom you love is ill" (11:1-3).

If the reader did not already know this story, the set-up would be confusing. First, the reader learns about a new character to this gospel, "a certain man" named Lazarus who was ill. Next readers learn the name of Lazarus' home town—Bethany, which can mean "house of affliction" or "house of the poor."[1] Then the reader is told of two other residents of Bethany: Mary and Martha. They, too, are new characters to this gospel. Readers learn that Mary was the one who anointed Jesus' feet, an act that does not occur until the next chapter (12:1–8). Next the narrator explains that it was Mary's brother, Lazarus, who was ill. In a round-about way, the reader figures out that if Mary and Lazarus are sister and brother, and if Mary and Martha are sisters, then this sign focuses on the story of these three siblings, who live in the same town. It seems such an unusual way to set up the story that will follow.

75

The narrator also sets up the story in various ways to link it with Jesus' own death. For example, the reference to Mary's anointing of Jesus is linked by Jesus to his death. A person's feet were usually only anointed at death. The feet of the living were regularly washed upon entering a house but not usually rubbed with oil, although this might be done for special guests at a banquet out of deep respect for the person.[2] The head of a live person might be anointed and not be an occasion for unusual notice. But in Jewish culture, feet were usually only anointed as part of a funeral preparation. When Mary performed this act and Judas challenged her lavish gift, Jesus said that she kept the perfume for the day of his burial. It was a difficult saying to grasp as Jesus sat there alive before them (12:7). But Jesus knew what only Mary seemed to understand—that his hour had come. The Fourth Gospel thus weaves together Lazarus' death and Jesus' death.

This gospel compels readers to read forward, then back again, to see connections between Jesus' seven signs and his "hour of glory," the term used to refer to the cross–resurrection section of this gospel. The Fourth Gospel clearly invites readers to do what each chapter of this present series has attempted to do: to recognise that each sign in its own way points to the most important moment, the hour of Jesus' death on the cross. Although Rome's way to shame and torture a criminal, for Jesus the cross will be a moment of being "lifted up" on behalf of the world and of bringing glory to God. To understand the implications of the story the writer wants us to notice the connections. This story is not only about Lazarus' death, it is also about Jesus' death.

A delayed arrival

At the end of John 10, we learned that Jesus had withdrawn from Jerusalem to a place beyond the Jordan where John the Baptist had first been baptising. Scholars think that this "Bethany beyond Jordan" was in a wadi just south of Galilee, the place of the brook Cherith. It was where Elijah had retreated when his life was threatened. Archaeologists have found ancient baptismal pools in the wadi. It is a place of contemplation and ministry, where Jesus had withdrawn when his own life was threatened (10:39, 40).[3] But many believed on him there (10:42). The link with the foreboding of death is unmistakable.

Having escaped to Bethany beyond the Jordan, Jesus received a message of distress from his friends in Bethany near Jerusalem. They wanted him to return. The sisters sent word to Jesus: "Lord, he whom you love is ill" (11:3).

During my sophomore year of college, my mother experienced some frightening physical symptoms that baffled her doctors. She spent quite a few days in the hospital undergoing tests. While she was there, a dear friend of ours sent her a card. Inside he wrote out John 11:3, modifying it just a little: "Lord, she whom you love is sick." It was such a comfort to my mother and to our family. During that scary time of illness, my mother had not been forgotten by God—and was not being punished by God. She was the one the Lord loved.

When Jesus heard the message from the sisters, he said, "This illness does not lead to death; rather it is for God's glory, so that the Son of God may be glorified through it" (11:4). These words from Jesus sound similar to his response to the disciples when they noticed but did not really see the man blind since birth (see Chapter 6). His blindness was so that God's work might be done through him. Like the blind man, Lazarus' illness would also help reveal God's glory. They are both signs, pointing ahead

The stories of the deaths of Jesus and Lazarus have been intentionally interwoven.

and revealing Jesus' identity. The stories of the deaths of Jesus and Lazarus have been intentionally interwoven. The author wants the reader to become increasingly aware of Jesus' death on the cross.

It is surprising that, "though Jesus loved Martha and her sister and Lazarus, after having heard that Lazarus was ill, he stayed two days longer in the place where he was" (11:5, 6). This description is similar to the description used when Jesus decided to stay two unplanned days with the Samaritans of the town of Sychar, the place where he met the woman at the well. In John 4:40, Jesus stayed that people might believe: "Many more did believe because of his word. They said to the woman, 'it is no longer because of what you said that we believe, for we have heard for ourselves, and we know that this is truly the Saviour of the world'" (4:41, 42).

But when Jesus extended his stay in the region of Samaria, a good friend was not dying. When Jesus stayed on in Samaria, two other good friends were not asking him for his presence elsewhere. And we, as readers, perhaps find ourselves upset with Jesus or, at least, we have questions for him.

This story also probably reflects how some of the first-century Christians felt as they watched loved ones get sick and die. Where are you, Jesus? You said you would return—soon. Why are you delaying? Where are you? Are You really coming back? As the years go by, all of us attend more and more funerals. We too have questions. Where are you, Jesus? Do you still hear us? Are you receiving our messages? Many of those you love are sick, Lord.

A journey toward death

After staying put for two days, Jesus suggests to his disciples that they go back to Judea again, specifically to the other Bethany, a town only about two kilometres (1.5 miles) from Jerusalem. The disciples think this is a bad idea. After all, the last time he was there, for the Feast of Tabernacles, people ended up trying to stone him (8:59). They protest. Jesus seems to hint that it is his duty—he must go—and then goes on to inform them: "Our friend Lazarus has fallen asleep, but I am going there to awaken him" (11:11).

Jesus went, even though the act of waking up Lazarus causes people to plot Jesus' death (11:45–53). Jesus went, even though Judea was a dangerous place and Jesus would not see Galilee again until after Golgotha. Jesus went, even though he walked toward the cross. Jesus went, because "No-one has greater love than this, to lay down one's life for one's friends" (15:13).

This part of the narrative contains further dialogue with significant double entendre, as the disciples misunderstand what Jesus meant about Lazarus having fallen asleep. So Jesus plainly states: "Lazarus is dead. For your sake I am glad I was not there, so that you may believe" (11:14, 15). At the end of the first sign, after Jesus changed water into wine, the narrator declared: "Jesus did this, the first of his signs . . . and revealed his glory; and his disciples believed in him" (2:11). At the end of Jesus' seventh sign, after Jesus changes a corpse into a living person, will the disciples believe? Will the readers of the Fourth Gospel believe?

The question lingers as Jesus makes his way to Bethany:

> When Jesus arrived, he found that Lazarus had already been in the tomb four days. . . . When Martha heard that Jesus was coming, she went and met him, while Mary stayed at home. Martha said to Jesus, "Lord, if you had been here, my brother would not have died. But even now I know that God will give you whatever you ask of him." Jesus said to her, "Your brother will rise again." Martha said to him, "I know that he will rise again in the resurrection on the last day" (11:17, 20–24).

The disciples who had travelled with Jesus to Bethany fade into the background of the story and three other disciples—Martha, Mary and Lazarus—come to the forefront. In her first words to Jesus, right there on the side of the road, Martha displayed a combination of emotions and convictions: regret, disappointment, anger, belief and hope. She believed she would see her brother again in the future, but she really missed him in the present.

When I worked as a pastor, I frequently sat with a person who had lost a loved one. One of my parishioners, who had recently lost his wife of 57 years, did not know what to say. Sometimes there is grief beyond words, even when you believe that "she will rise again in the resurrection on the last day."

Jesus said to Martha: "I AM the resurrection and the life. Those who believe in me, even though they die, will live, and everyone who lives and believes in me will never die" (11:25, 26). The life Jesus was offering in this gospel was a *present* reality in him. Lazarus being raised was proof of this reality, but it would still be true about Jesus had Lazarus remained in the grave. John's gospel was claiming that eternal life is a present reality; that it is true when our loved ones remain in the grave. Jesus is the resurrection and the life! Death—still an enemy—is a *defeated* foe! Death does *not* have the last word.

Jesus asked Martha: "Do you believe this?" She said to him, "Yes, Lord, I believe that you are the Messiah, the Son of God, the one coming into the world" (11:27).

Martha's confession of belief is similar to John's purpose statement at the end of the gospel: "These are written that you may continue to believe that Jesus is the Messiah, the Son of God, and that by believing, you may have life in his name" (20:31). Martha returned to their home and told Mary that Jesus was making his way to them. The narrator then describes Mary as quickly getting up and going out to meet Jesus. Her eagerness highlights her anguish.

Experiences of grief

Immediately following a burial, Jewish custom required that the women of the family return home to mourn for 30 days. While in mourning, they sat on the floor of their home. When Mary heard that Jesus was calling for her, she left the floor and went out to Jesus. When she saw him, Mary burst out with the same phrase her sister had used: "Lord, if you had been here, my brother would not have died."

This time, rather than a conversation about the resurrection, Jesus was moved: "When Jesus saw her weeping, and the Jews who came with her also weeping, he was greatly disturbed in spirit and deeply moved" (11:32, 33).

The words here in the original language are almost untranslatable. Jesus was "greatly disturbed in spirit" or he "groaned in his spirit."[4] It will be repeated in a few verses and it gives the idea of deep anger. Picture a whole body shudder of grief, as when a horse snorts. Jesus is very angry. And Jesus is "deeply moved" or "deeply troubled." It is the same word used for the "stirring up of the water" (5:7) at the pool in Bethesda. Jesus was troubled; he is stirring. The pool of living water is stirring.

Jesus asked, "Where have you laid him?" They said to him, "Lord, come and see" (11:34). Once again, the narrative anticipates Jesus' death. "Come and see" was the phrase used by Jesus to invite the first disciples to see where he is going (1:38, 39). Now it is "come and see" a tomb. Then Scripture says: "Jesus began to weep. So the Jews said, 'See how he loved him!' But some of them said, 'Could not he who opened the eyes of the blind man have kept this man from dying?'" (11:35–37).

The author is carefully building the sense of anticipation. Earlier Jesus had said: "Our friend Lazarus has fallen asleep, but I am going there to awaken him" (11:11). First-time readers might wonder: can Jesus wake someone up from the dead? Is death like sleep to Jesus? Is it like opening the eyes of the blind man or curing crippled legs?

And if so, why did Jesus weep? Was he weeping because of all that was being misunderstood? Was he weeping because the sign he was about to do would cause the wrath of the Jews to fall upon him, Lazarus and all who believed? Was he weeping because of those who chose death rather than life?

Jesus groaned again—that sound of deep anger.

Giving Life

After going to the tomb—a cave with a stone in front of it—Jesus said:

> "Take away the stone." Martha, the sister of the dead man, said to him, "Lord, already there is a stench because he has been dead four days." Jesus said to her, "Did I not tell you that if you believed, you would see the glory of God?" (11:39, 40).

Many Jews believed the soul of a person remained with the body for three days after death. But by the fourth day, the person was irretrievably gone; the body was no longer human. Moreover, even a body wrapped up carefully, lovingly and anointed with much perfume would nevertheless be overcome with the smell of decay after four days.

As the people lifted the stone and rolled it back, Jesus lifted his eyes and looked skyward:

> "Father, I thank you for having heard me. I knew that you always hear me, but I have said this for the sake of the crowd standing here, so that they may believe that you sent me." When he had said this, he cried with a loud voice: "Lazarus, come out!" (11:41–43).

We should pause to notice some other connections the author of this Fourth Gospel hopes we will make with the previous discussion in Chapter 10. Before Jesus learned of Lazarus' illness, Jesus had given a discourse on the actions of the Good Shepherd. Unlike false shepherds, a good shepherd "calls his own sheep by name and leads them out. When he has brought out all his own, he goes ahead of them, and the sheep follow him because they know his voice" (10:3, 4). Will Lazarus know Jesus' voice? Will Lazarus hear his name called by the Good Shepherd? Will Lazarus be led out of the tomb?

Much earlier in the gospel—after the third sign—when those in the temple challenged Jesus and questioned his authority to heal and tell a man to carry his mat on the Sabbath, Jesus further infuriated them by claiming that: "Very truly, I tell you, the hour is coming, and is now here, when the dead will hear the voice of the Son of God, and those who hear will live" (5:25). Jesus responded to their accusation of blasphemy by further associating himself with the work of divinity: "Do not be astonished at this; for the hour is coming when all who are in their graves will hear his voice and will come out" (5:28, 29).

Suddenly, the claims Jesus has already made throughout this gospel come true: "The dead man came out" (11:44). The dead man came out of the grave, "his hands and feet bound with strips of cloth, and his face wrapped in a cloth. Jesus said to them, 'Unbind him, and let him go'" (11:44).

If we want details about this miracle, if we want to know what Lazarus remembered, how he got from the tomb to outside, how quickly people unwrapped him, what he first said to his sisters, we will be disappointed. In this gospel, the mechanics of the signs—the how and the why and the wherefore—are never the main point. The signs in the Fourth Gospel have one major purpose: to reveal Jesus' true identity. They point to Jesus, and the hour of his greatest sign of all: when Jesus' death led to life. This sign was not only about Lazarus dying and rising again. This sign pointed to Jesus dying and rising again.

The reactions

As readers have come to expect, the sign of Lazarus' resurrection resulted in two striking reactions from those who witnessed it: one group believed in Jesus; the other plotted to kill him. At the end of John 11, the Jewish leadership plots Jesus' death (11:47–53), even as Mary prepares Jesus' body for burial by anointing his feet with perfume (12:1–8).

Mary's act anticipates when Jesus' body was taken from the cross and two other disciples carefully wrapped it using an enormous amount of spices in the linen cloths (19:40). They then placed the body in a tomb, which was covered by a stone. But note the similarities between the two stories, the two burials, the two resurrections.

Lazarus—whose name means "God helps"—was in a tomb, behind a stone, wrapped in linen cloths. Mary, his sister, was weeping. Jesus said: "I AM the resurrection and the life!" Then, calling his disciple by name, Jesus said: "Lazarus, come out!" And the community was called to unbind him.

Jesus—whose name means "Jehovah saves"—was in a tomb, behind a stone, wrapped in linen cloths. Mary Magdalene was weeping. The I AM resurrected! Then, calling his disciple by name, Jesus said: "Mary." Jesus didn't need help with the linen cloths. He was completely free of death's wrappings. John even mentions that the cloth for Jesus' head was rolled up (20:7). And Jesus tells Mary to go to the community and begin telling the good news of Jesus' triumph over death. Here is the part of John's story to which every sign has been pointing.

Initially, Mary wants to hold onto Jesus. But the resurrected Jesus is offering a new relationship to all who believe. He is "ascending to my Father and your Father, to my God and your God" (20:17). Through Jesus, that oneness between Father and Son extends to all who believe in him. Jesus' disciples can experience a new kind of relationship *with God*.

Signs to life

For the Fourth Gospel, all seven signs lead to this new life possible through belief in Jesus.

- This gospel invites each thirsty reader to drink the wine of abundant life and to know the source of the transformation.
- Each reader is challenged to hear the words spoken by the Word and to believe even before seeing the sign.
- This gospel challenges readers to feel the stirring of the water of life energising our crippled limbs and renewing our crippled hearts.
- Readers are invited to eat of the Bread of Life, which is the flesh and blood of Jesus, the true manne from heaven.
- This gospel reassures readers as Jesus, the I AM, says: "Do not be afraid."
- This gospel offers to open our eyes by focusing its story on the Light of the World.
- And this gospel invites us to experience resurrection life.

For the Fourth Gospel, all these possibilities—transformations and belief, wholeness and healing, Eucharist, fearlessness, new insight and resurrection—may be experienced not only in the future at Jesus' return, but also in the present, through the spirit of Jesus among the community of faith.

Consider your response to the Fourth Gospel—to this Good News— as you read a passage from the beginning of this gospel:

> And the Word became flesh and lived among us, and we have seen his glory, the glory as of a father's only son, full of grace and truth. . . . From his fullness we have all received, grace upon grace. The law indeed was given through Moses; grace and truth came through Jesus Christ. No-one has ever seen God. It is God the only Son, who is close to the Father's heart, who has made him known (1:14–18).

And at the end of this story, Jesus said to Mary: "Go to my brothers and say to them, 'I am ascending to my Father and your Father, to My God and your God'" (20:17).

Adventist Christians believe that because of the wonder of the Word made flesh and because of the glory of his cross, because of Mary's witness to Jesus' resurrection and because Jesus has ascended to God, we face a future in the fullness of God's presence.

1. Raymond E Brown, *The Gospel According to John I-XII*, The Anchor Bible series, Garden City, NY: Doubleday & Company, Inc, 1966, page 422.

2. Bruce J Malina and Richard L Rohrbaugh, *Social-Science Commentary on the Gospel of John*, Minneapolis, MN: Fortress Press, 1998, page 205. See also the lengthy discussion of the scene in Philip F Esler and Ronald Piper, *Lazarus, Mary and Martha: Social-Scientific Approaches to the Gospel of John*, Minneapolis, MN: Fortress Press, 2006, especially pages 64–74 and Appendix 2.

3. It is also the place to which early Christians retreated when they escaped from the destruction of Jerusalem in AD 70.

4. See discussion by Raymond E Brown, *The Gospel According to John I-XII*, The Anchor Bible series, Garden City, NY: Doubleday & Company, Inc, 1966, pages 425–6.

Part II

Abundant Life

READERS RESPOND

From Sorrow To Joy

Carolyn Rickett

It is writers rather than boyscouts who must investigate the

culture of knots, learn

to pitch words by the sea, to make

fire with less than two vowels rubbed together

and name it other than the groan of despair.

—Janet Frame, "Beach"

Being

In her poem "Beach," Janet Frame alludes to the capacity of writers to create and produce meaningful texts that might then be interpreted by a reader as a form of meaning, nourishment and inspiration. What appeals to me about the gospel of John is that the writer ultimately presents a contemporary reader with something beyond the "groan of despair" even though despair has been audible throughout many of his stories.

The earlier chapters of this book have highlighted a number of Jesus' encounters and stories marked by longing and loss. As an academic with a background in literature and communication, my recent research has taken me into the area of medical humanities where I have an interest in what storytelling can offer people in crisis. From this context,

I come to the stories narrated by John and what they might say about the grief we experience when someone we love dies.

It is significant that in the opening verses of this gospel there is an assertion of ultimate healing and hope through Christ: "What has come into being in him was life, and the life was the light of all people. The light shines in the darkness, and the darkness did not overcome it" (1:4, 5). Importantly, the reader is reassured from the outset that whatever "darkness" they will navigate in the stories that follow and in the wider context of their own lived reality, those who believe in and receive Christ can become children of God. However, to be a child of God does not mean being exempt from tragedy, but it does mean physical or psychic suffering is not all we will ultimately experience.

Biblical scholar René Kieffer suggests the gospel of John is framed around a series of binary oppositions: "The Johannine presentation is permeated with contrasts between light and darkness, life and death, truth and falsehood, heaven above and earth below."[1] Reading this particular gospel from my 21st-century perspective, these core tensions present some of the most difficult thematic challenges in the text. The particular contrasts that Kieffer refers to raise the seemingly insurmountable questions: *How do we patiently wait for the promise of heaven while experiencing and witnessing acute suffering on earth? How do we embrace life to the full when we are shadowed by death?*

Because there are no easy or evident answers, it becomes a structural priority for the writer of this gospel to make a key distinction in the first chapter that the children of God are "born not of blood or of the will of the flesh or of the will of man, but of God" (1:13). This affirmation works in part as a preparatory reassurance that to be born of God is to be afforded something more than human fragility and mortality. It is a bidding to live consciously *now* with the certain prospect of eternal life in the future. Yet the assurance of future longevity does not protect against the harrowing impact of present losses.

The writer of John intuitively knows our temporality will be traced by the sorrow that comes from being physically separated by the death of someone we love. So we are tasked with navigating the paradoxical promise of future life in the midst of present death/s. Such a promise might moderate a long-term grief trajectory, but might not readily alleviate an original experience of intense suffering. In order to help us understand that reactions to loss are multifaceted, Therese Rando explains: "Grief is experienced in each of three major ways—psychologically (through your feelings, thoughts and attitudes), socially (through your behaviour with others) and physically (through your health and bodily symptoms)."[2] In this sense, grief can be all encompassing.

This kind of consuming response to losing someone we love can be made even more problematic because it is rare for us today to see the instantaneous intervention and healing such as that given by Jesus to the official's son, to the cripple at the pool or to a person born blind. Instead, more frequent are the desperate prayers offered in doctors' surgeries as someone waits for confirmation of a terminal diagnosis gleaned from a biopsy; exhausted prayers offered beside hospital beds as machines beep and breathe for a patient who is no longer cognisant; and prayers gradually weakened by a perceived silence from God. And, when we finally stand at a graveside, a stark contrast forms between the miracle offered to a family in Capernaum—"Go; your son will live" (4:50)—and our own bereavement occasioned by an unhalted death. During such times, we are easily returned to a familiar scene in Lamentations where "the joy of our hearts has ceased; [and] our dancing has been turned to mourning" (Lamentations 5:15).

Waiting

In his presentation of stories, it is as if John understood that while narratives of instant healing might encourage and promote spiritual belief for some people, such narratives can also be potentially discouraging when we find Jesus not enacting the same speedy cure for a life-threatening illness when we pray for the same kind of divine sign. Why doesn't it happen to us? While the writer of this gospel signals Jesus' desire to stop and heal those in physical and emotional crisis, the story of Lazarus offers me most insight about dealing with loss and grief when a prayer for healing is not immediately answered.

Along with the account of Lazarus' death are references to attempts of the Pharisees to undermine Jesus' authority (see John 5:18; 6:52; 7:32; 8:48; 9:16; 10:33) and the distressing prediction of his death (see John 5:20; 6:71; 8:21; 11:53; 12:7, 8; 13:27; 13:33–36). However, the darker elements of such betrayals sit alongside Jesus' robust claim: "I am the light of the world. Whoever follows me will never walk in darkness but will have the light of life" (8:12). Declarations like this no doubt prompted Mary and Martha's unflagging belief that the dire message sent to Jesus about their brother's illness would be met with an astonishing sign of curing.

Their message is made all the more moving by the fact that Lazarus has a deep connection with Jesus: "Lord, he whom you love is ill" (11:3). These simple words form a pressing lacuna for Jesus' power to fill, a gap where his authority can readily disperse darkness. These words function as an invitation for Jesus to perform again the instant miracle of recuperation and restoration. His capacity for performing wondrous signs throughout his ministry is already common knowledge to the sisters (11:21, 32) and even the larger community (11:37). Jesus' ability to restore bodily deficit has become one of the features of his ministry. Mary and Martha are keenly aware that a key motivation in Jesus healing someone is to reverse the stigmatised position of the ill or disabled person within a prejudicial cultural context.[3]

We are told that, when Jesus had received the sisters' message, he replied with the ambiguous words: "This illness does not lead to death; rather it is for God's glory, so that the son of God may be glorified through it" (11:4). Jesus signals an optimism not evident to any other onlooker. He does not seem troubled by the urgency of the medical crisis being played out in Bethany. Most perplexing for Mary and Martha is that, after he hears about the ominous situation, Jesus stays where he is for another two days. On a first reading, one might think Jesus has not comprehended the gravity of the situation and is strategically using the situation of a personal catastrophe to underscore a religious point.

Unsurprising to the reader though, Lazarus dies, the anticipated moment of possible healing is denied by the plot and Jesus' absence is duly noted. At this point, the inconsolable mourners waiting in Bethany are not privy to the intentions Jesus reveals to his disciples: "Our friend Lazarus has fallen asleep, but I am going to waken him" (11:11). The word "sleep" is interpreted literally by the disciples who fail to read it as a euphemism for death, so Jesus needs to speak plainly to them in a way that removes any obscurity: "Lazarus is dead. For your sake I am glad I was not there, so that you may believe. But let us go to him" (11:14, 15).

It is easy to construct an initial reading of this scene as Jesus' calculated decision to delay so a resurrection miracle will dispel any doubt about his identity as the Son of God. Juxtaposed with this more triumphant reading is what might also appear to some readers as a lack of any strong empathic engagement with the trauma Mary and Martha face. While they are consumed by personal grief, Jesus seems to be working systematically and collectively toward a proof of his divinity.

The reader knows Lazarus had already been buried for four days when Jesus arrives in Bethany. Lazarus is not asleep; he is now a corpse. This is such a confronting image because a corpse is one of the most alienating and abject figurations from which we naturally recoil. In her influential essay *Powers of Horror*, Julia Kristeva explains that her reading of the abject is linked to the human reaction a person has when meaning is threatened by the loss of distinguishable boundaries between the self (subject) and other (object). Her principal illustration of this is the horror a person experiences when first looking at a corpse. In such an encounter, the trauma of directly confronting human materiality heightens a person's feeling of vulnerability. As Kristeva notes, "The corpse, seen without God and outside of science, is the utmost of abjection. It is death infecting life. Abject."[4]

What we have in Bethany is this breakdown of boundaries. The neat demarcations between the oppositional states of health/disease and life/death are now conflated, if not feared. Death has infected life. Feeling the physical absence of a redemptive healer, it would have been difficult for Mary and Martha to process what Lazarus has now so quickly and irreversibly become.

Hoping

Jesus' absence at this crisis becomes even more pronounced when John records the comparative presence of others who have come to acknowledge the sisters' loss: "Many of the Jews had come to Mary and Martha to console them about their brother" (11:19). It can be troubling for a reader to find the Jews there but see no active evidence of Jesus comforting them at a time of such intense grief.

When Martha leaves the house to meet Jesus in transit, her first words to him carry the weight of our own questions: "Lord, if you had been here, my brother would not have died" (11:21). By addressing him as "Lord," her first act is to acknowledge his divinity and her second act is to point out—because of his power over darkness—that he could have preserved Lazarus' life. However, it is not an embittered comment because she says that even now, in the present moment of encounter, God will give Jesus "whatever you ask of him" (11:22).

Jesus' reply to Martha is unwaveringly assured: "Your brother will rise again" (11:23). As a contemporary reader of the New Testament, these words transport me to an evocation in 1 Thessalonians which resonates with similar reassurance: "For the Lord himself, with a cry of command, with the archangel's call and with the sound of God's trumpet, will descend from heaven, and the dead in Christ will rise first" (1 Thessalonians 4:16).

Martha understands an eschatology that includes a future resurrection. She quickly responds: "I know that he will rise in the resurrection on the last day" (11:24). She already declares knowledge of some future hope, but what matters most to Jesus in this conversation is to bring the concept of something delayed and far off into a contemporaneous meeting with the source of light: "I am the resurrection and the life. Those who believe in me, even though they die, will live, and everyone who lives and believes in me will never die" (11:25, 26).

Jesus then moves from the general to the specific, asking Martha whether she believes in this redemptive prospect: "Do *you* believe this?" (11:26, emphasis mine). His question is also a call to the reader to reflect on his or her own belief about the transience of human life and whether—like Martha—we can imagine the option of something beyond human extinction. Martha bears witness to a faith that appears to help her deal with her grief: "Yes, Lord, I believe that you are the Messiah, the Son of God, the one coming into the world" (11:27).

After this declaration, Martha returns home to Mary to pass on a private message that Jesus wants to see her. Mary quickly goes to where Jesus has just met with Martha and, in an act I simultaneously read as both worship and despair, she kneels at his feet and echoes her sister's initial consternation: "Lord, if you had been here, my brother would not have died" (11:32). Her present grief has been complicated by the fact she knows Jesus had the power to prevent this family tragedy.

Like Martha's, Mary's response to him is one of perplexed distress. Her opening sentence works as a potent re-echoing of Martha's first words of human encounter with the divine: "If you had been here . . ." the catastrophe could have been averted. "If you . . ."—the One who can turn water into wine, heal a dying son, rescue a chronically ill man by a pool in Bethesda, feed 5000 people with nothing more than five barley loaves and two fish, walk across raging water to comfort the disciples in a storm, restore a blind man's sight—"If only *you* had been there . . ."

Readers can easily identify with her unsaid interrogation: *Where were you when I needed you to save my brother?* When Mary weeps words for Jesus' perceived absence, she weeps for the cavern between the promise of a forthcoming resurrection and the current severing of a familial bond. She weeps because, despite his claims of omnipotence, Jesus seems to have been deliberately tardy. He knew how sick Lazarus was. They got the message to him. So where had he been? How could he do nothing? Why would he stay away when he is most needed? What could be more important than preventing their loss? Even "the Jews" have made an effort to come and sit with her—and Jesus is only turning up now, days too late.

> **When Mary weeps words for Jesus' perceived absence, she weeps for the cavern between the promise of a forthcoming resurrection and the current severing of a familial bond.**

What is powerfully affecting is the way that John has sequenced this story: Martha's testimony that she believes wholeheartedly in Christ—the Son of God, who promises victory over death—is followed by the heart-wrenching encounter Jesus has with Mary. What is encouraging is that even though there is an overarching assurance in Martha's affirmation that Jesus can conquer death, we are also brought into the sacred place of a truly human grief reaction so palpably portrayed through Mary's sense of abandonment. In this haunting posture of part exhaustion and part prayer, she presents Jesus with her unassuaged sorrow.

Jesus, who until this point in the narrative appears to have been more theologically focused, models to us what I consider to be one of the most profound reactions to bereavement in the Bible. The writer of John captures the moment this way: "When Jesus saw her weeping, and the Jews coming with her also weeping, he was greatly disturbed in spirit and deeply moved" (11:33). Instead of offering Mary glib platitudes about God's ultimate will, Jesus understands the impact and magnitude of an immediate loss—both theirs and his. Jesus' response helps perform the important work of normalising human grief. The authors of *The Grief Recovery Handbook* write of the importance of acknowledging the appropriateness of grief when reacting to loss:

> Grief is the normal reaction to loss of any kind. . . . While grief is normal and natural, and clearly the most powerful of all emotions, it is also the most neglected and misunderstood experience, often by both the grievers and those around them.[5]

Becoming

While Jesus' impulse is to rectify the situation by asking where Lazarus' tomb is, what is most significant is the writer highlighting the importance of expressing feelings of his extreme sadness: "Jesus began to weep" (11:35). Jesus well knows that resurrections are not only possible but assured, but is still affected deeply by the gravity of death. He allows himself to feel the pain of what it means relationally for a human life to have tangibly disappeared from view, and what it feels like to no longer be able to talk to or touch the embodied presence of love. In that weeping pause between death and resurrection, Jesus demonstrates the importance of stopping to contemplate and share our own and others' grief. Even with a sense of future hope, human reactions to loss are valid.

In recounting Jesus' weeping reaction to loss, I am reminded of the moving observation Dr H Norman Wright makes about Jesus' desire to alleviate physical and psychic distress:

> The compassion he felt was obviously quite different from superficial or passing feelings of sorrow or sympathy. Rather,

it extended to the most vulnerable part of his being. It related to the Hebrew word *rachamin*, which refers to the womb of Yahweh. . . . He became lost with the lost, hungry with the hungry, and sick with the sick. In him, all suffering was sensed with a perfect sensitivity.[6]

The writer of John highlights this kind of sensitivity when he depicts Jesus, again, being "greatly disturbed" (11:38) by what confronts him when he goes to Lazarus' tomb—a cave with a stone covering the entrance. The burden of death is literally and metaphorically represented by the intransigent rock covering access to their loved one. What is beautifully rendered at the close of this particular story is Jesus' calling Lazarus to life, inviting him to walk out of the dark cave and into light. Jesus says to those passively witnessing the resurrection: "Unbind him, and let him go" (11:44).

What I imagine also happening here is a symbolic invitation to Martha and Mary to unbind their grief and embrace the prospect of a new life, most immediately their brother's, and ultimately the inheritance of eternal life offered to all who believe in the risen Christ. Later he uttered the memorable assurance: "Very truly I tell you, you will weep and mourn . . . you will have pain, but your pain will turn into joy" (16:20). These words function as prelude and preparation for the grief the disciples are about to experience. They form the narrative trajectory of the gospel of John, moving from the harrowing experience of Lazarus dying to the betrayal, arrest, crucifixion and burial of Jesus. The resurrection of both Lazarus and Jesus testify to the promise and lived experience of re-connection after death.

We are told that Mary Magdalene stood "weeping outside the tomb" (20:11). In her state of deep grief, she is unable to recognise the risen Christ standing before her. Jesus asks her, "Woman, why are you weeping? Whom are you looking for?" (20:15) With her perception clouded by unremitting sorrow, Mary has not yet apprehended the reality that Jesus has finally conquered death. When she does recognise him as her Messiah and not a gardener at the site of the tomb, she completes the important mission of announcing his resurrection to the disciples: "I have seen the Lord" (20:18).

It is vital that Jesus then appears to his disciples so they, too, can experience a personal reunion and testify to Jesus' claim that there is ultimate victory over death for those who believe in the Son of God. In fact, the writer of John reveals the main reason the stories have been recorded in the gospel is "so that you may come to believe that Jesus is the Messiah, the Son of God, and that through believing you might have life in his name" (20:31).

When I read this verse through an interdisciplinary lens it forms a stark and poignant contrast with some of the final remarks made by French philosopher and writer Jacques Derrida. In the last interview he gave before his death, Derrida confessed:

> I never learned-to-live. In fact not at all! Learning to live should mean learning to die, learning to take into account, so as to accept, absolute mortality that is without salvation, resurrection or redemption—neither for oneself nor for the other.[7]

The writer of John's gospel offers an alternative view. He demonstrates that learning to live will involve the painful process of learning to see death as a destructive part of human life, but the prospect of salvation and resurrection offers us joy beyond grief. However, if we are tempted to see such a promise as an easy fix to the demanding and important work of mourning loss, William Worden's research on current theories of how grief is processed provides a useful insight. He sees the work of mourning involving the following challenging tasks: (1) to accept the reality of the loss; (2) to process the pain of grief; and (3) to adjust to a world without the deceased.[8]

This kind of protracted emotional work and the demanding process of responding to the "changed world" and re-creating a new one after the death of a loved one is something I believe the gospel of John identifies with. In partly answering the important question—*How do the bereaved overcome their loss?*[9]—we find in this gospel that Jesus' actions are motivated by the importance of building a kinship of people who are prepared to recognise and share in each other's suffering. In each of the stories that pivot around loss, Jesus finds a way to directly connect with people, rather than leaving them distressed and isolated.

Belonging

From my reading, the writer of John is deeply interested in strategies that enable us to work through grief in a way that helps us find a "path into the future."[10] The empathic way Jesus listened to people whose faith and philosophical systems were being challenged by physical and psychological pain is a reminder of one of the fundamental ways to helpfully respond to grief, which is to validate it. In Darian Leader's work on mourning, he makes these important points: "As humans, don't we need others to authenticate our losses? To recognise them as losses rather than to pass over them in silence?"[11]

Jesus went about the work of recognising losses, modelling a form of healing ministry to us—to stop and acknowledge another person's suffering rather than swiftly offer trite and condescending clichés. His actions show that the true work of community involves being present to the stories of others, valuing and recognising the role that listening to and creating narratives can play. In her work on how sharing each other's stories can be a transformative and healing act, Louise de Salvo writes of the social rituals we have for supporting people through the process of grieving and loss: "As we come together to mourn, we assert our need for community, for having others recognise the magnitude of what we've experienced, the emotional journey we've traversed."[12]

Through the stories of Lazarus' death and Jesus' own crucifixion, Jesus is saying something important about traversing human geography: "I know what darkness looks like, I have been there myself and have wept." He wept because he wanted to show us something of the depth of grief and perhaps to give us permission to simultaneously feel the kind of sorrow that can coexist with hope—or, in his words, "light." I think he wept to signify the complex nature of grief, as if to remind us there are no easy theological solutions to a primal reaction to loss. And we know from current practitioners who work in this field that there are patterns of grief that need to be more carefully understood when we are ministering to ourselves and other people. The three patterns of grief might be described in the following way:

> The first, called *common* grief, is marked by an initial increase in distress following a death; the distress abates slowly with time. The second pattern, *chronic* grief, is marked by high distress following a death, and this distress remains high over time. And the third pattern, *delayed* grief, is marked by low distress after a death, with a rise in distress at some later point.[13]

By appreciating the different kinds of distress and patterns of grief when listening to other people's stories, Jesus asks us to take part in the kind of healing that only comes into being through community.

The key questions remain: *How do we patiently wait for the promise of a heaven while experiencing and witnessing acute suffering on earth? How do we embrace life to the full when we are shadowed by death?* While we may find that we do not always wait with complete answers, we can wait with and comfort each other. In the liminal spaces between darkness and full light, between cemeteries and resurrections, Jesus invites us to participate in his ethic of care, which enacts one of the most extraordinary miracles of all: "I give you a new commandment, that you love one another. Just as I have loved you, you should also love one another" (13:34).

1. René Kieffer in John Muddiman and John Barton (editors), *The Gospels*, New York: Oxford University Press, 2010, page 186.

2. Therese Rando, *How to Go On Living When Someone You Loves Dies*. New York: Bantam Books, 1991, page 12.

3. Comparatively speaking, Arthur Kleinman's work on reading the ill body demonstrates some of the perceptions that still persist today: "Stigma often carries a religious significance—the afflicted person is viewed as sinful or evil—or a moral connotation of weakness and dishonour." He argues that the "stigmatised person" can often be "defined as alien other, upon whose persona are projected the attributes the group regards as opposite to the ones it values." See Arthur Kleinman, *The Illness Narratives: Suffering, Healing and the Human Condition*, Basic Books, 1998, page 159.

4. Julia Kristeva, *Powers of Horror: An Essay on Abjection* (translated Leon S Roudiez), New York: Columbia University Press, 1982, page 4.

5. John W James and Russell Friedman, *The Grief Recovery Handbook*, New York: William Morrow, 2009, page 3.

6. H Norman Wright, *The Complete Guide to Crisis & Trauma Counseling: What to Do and Say When It Matters Most*, California: Regal, 2011, page 18.

7. Jacques Derrida, *Learning to Live Finally: The Last Interview* (translated Pascale-Anne Brault and Michael Naas), Hoboken, NJ: Melville House Publishing, 2007, page 24.

8. J William Worden, *Grief Counseling and Grief Therapy: A Handbook for the Mental Health Practitioner* (Fourth Edition), New York: Springer Publishing Company, 2009, page 37.

9. Wright, op cit, page 248.

10. ibid.

11. Darian Leader, *The New Black: Mourning, Melancholia and Depression*, London: Penguin Books, 2008, page 85.

12. Louise De Salvo, *Writing as a Way of Healing: How Telling Our Stories Transforms Our Lives*, New York: Harper Collins, 1999, page 209.

13. Melissa M Kelley, *Grief: Contemporary Theory and the Practice of Ministry*, MN: Fortress Press, 2010, page 16.

The Enigma of Jesus in the Gospel of John

Daniel Reynaud

The gospel of John is one of my favourite Bible books. I love its imagery and tone. It feels like a text steeped in warmth and love. It uses simple and concrete language, yet this simplicity is rich in profound meaning.

At the same time, however, I find it a most frustrating text, wrapped in mystery, riddle and irony. Pivotal to this sense of frustration is the character of Jesus himself, who stands as the central enigma: time and again, John the Evangelist portrays him as puzzling to his audience, uttering statements that confound his listeners. With the benefit of decades of hindsight, the author adds some explanatory comments— but not always.

With my background in literature—the literature of the Bible, in particular—it fascinates me that a character could be portrayed with such irony. He offers himself as the answer to the great questions of life, yet he presents himself as so mysterious that many people—even his closest followers—fail to understand him. Typically when Jesus speaks within the narrative, his words increase the mystery rather than give clarity. How am I to understand this conundrum of The Answer providing yet more mystery?

As a student of literature, I know irony is an important literary device used by an author to make a vital point. So I must assume the irony is deliberate, designed to push me beyond the obvious level of meaning to what the Evangelist wants me to understand that Jesus is really saying and meaning. In his introduction to a discussion of irony, Alan Culpepper suggests that there is a "silent" communication at work between author and reader and that this "assumes its most intriguing form in the ironies of the gospel." He suggests that the author "smiles, winks and raises his eyebrows as the story is told. The reader who sees as well as hears understands that the narrator means more than he says." It also means that the characters may not always understand what is happening or even what they are saying.[1] Other scholars have noted John's extensive use of ambiguous words, misunderstandings, riddles and irony as key elements in presenting his message.[2] With this idea in the back of my mind then, I began to apply literary analysis skills to explore the ironies in the enigmatic portrayal of Jesus in the gospel of John.

The temple

The presence of this ironic enigma first struck me when reading the story of the cleansing of the temple, one of the early narratives of the gospel of John. After Jesus drives the merchants out of the temple courts, his disciples remember the prophecy, "Zeal for your house will consume me" (2:17). The quotation from Psalm 69:9 is not one an ordinary reader would anticipate as a messianic prophecy. But like so many of the prophetic fulfilments in the other gospels, only hindsight makes it possible to discern prophetic revelation. When challenged by the religious leaders over what authority he had to take such actions, Jesus enigmatically proclaims, "Destroy this temple, and in three days I will raise it up" (2:19). The leaders do not understand—and take the statement literally.

Jesus must know that his claim is ambiguous; in fact, it is deliberately so. But why should he make such a statement? It opens him to ridicule, disbelief and even a potentially case-clinching accusation at his trial (as reported in Matthew 26:61 and Mark 14:58). Only hindsight can make sense of the statement, and the Evangelist explains at this point: "But he was speaking of the temple of his body" (2:21). He then adds,

101

"After he was raised from the dead, his disciples remembered that he had said this; and they believed the scripture and the word that Jesus had spoken" (2:22).

Here is the clue that helped me make sense of Jesus' riddle—one of the most overt cases in the gospel of John of this kind of ironic enigma. The Evangelist portrays Jesus as having no intention that his audience will understand his words at the time he utters them. Jesus spoke prophetically, revealing his true nature. The revelation's meaning, however, was hidden in a riddle that could only be understood after the occurrence of the events to which it referred. In other words, the purpose of the prophecy was not to forewarn the disciples so that they would be prepared for coming events. Rather, it was to confirm their trust in him after the event.

Jesus' foreknowledge

One also finds a cluster of occurrences in the Farewell Speech (13:1–17:26). At the final Passover, for example, Jesus makes a series of related statements with a similar theme. After washing the disciples' feet, Jesus again speaks in riddles: "'And you are clean, though not all of you.' For he knew who was to betray him; for this reason he said, 'Not all of you are clean'" (13:10, 11). The author intrudes again to explain in hindsight what was at the time another enigmatic statement.

Soon after, speaking of his betrayer again, Jesus says, "But it is to fulfil the scripture, the one who ate my bread has lifted his heel against me. I tell you this now, before it occurs, so that when it does occur, you may believe that I am he" (13:18, 19). Here, Jesus plainly announces the purpose of his prophetic riddle: a prophecy being fulfilled before their eyes was not something the disciples were expected to recognise as it happened, so this prophecy was not intended to forewarn. Instead, its function was to confirm *post-factum* the foreknowledge of Jesus as evidence of his divine character.

Twice more the same idea is repeated in this extended farewell speech of Jesus. In 16:4, Jesus says, "But I have said these things to you so that when their hour comes you may remember that I told you about them." Then in 16:33, Jesus says, "I have said this to you, so that in me you may have peace." His outlining of the future is designed to bring the assurance, not that the disciples would have every detail of the future worked out, but that they could trust that Jesus knew and had everything under control. It was not in the prophecy that they were to have peace, but rather in Jesus.

Johannine irony

We have noticed four statements spread across an entire Gospel at its beginning and its end. But is this making a mountain out of a molehill? Not at all. Although in less overt form, similar themes are consistently present throughout the gospel. Some scholars refer to the characteristic as "Johannine irony." Repeatedly, the gospel's author records riddles and enigmatic statements associated with Jesus that baffle his audiences, despite Jesus' insistence on making clear his own identity and his relationship to the Father. And where people believe, it is usually after they had seen a "sign"—as miracles are usually termed in the gospel. A quick glance shows the density of such events. There is quite a list I can mention.[3]

The gospel of John begins with metaphors evoking mystery and incomprehension: "The light shines in the darkness, and the darkness did not overcome it" (1:5). John the Baptist testifies at Jesus' baptism that he did not know who Jesus was until after he saw the Holy Spirit descend on him (1:33, 34).

To Nathaniel, Jesus says, "Do you believe because I told you that I saw you under the fig tree? You will see greater things than these" (1:50). He then prophesies, "Very truly, I tell you, you will see heaven opened and the angels of God ascending and descending upon the Son of Man" (1:51), a statement that almost certainly meant little to his listeners until later.

At the Cana wedding, the master is in ignorance of the origin of the fine wine, though the servants who witnessed the miracle know (2:9): "Jesus did this, the first of his signs, in Cana of Galilee, and revealed his glory; and his disciples believed in him" (2:11).

In 2:23, 24, "many believed in his name because they saw the signs that he was doing. But Jesus on his part would not entrust himself to them, because he knew all people." Similarly, Jesus berates Nicodemus, "Very truly, I tell you, we speak of what we know and testify to what we have seen; yet you do not receive our testimony. If I have told you about earthly things and you do not believe, how can you believe if I tell you about heavenly things?" (3:11, 12). By contrast, the Samaritans believed because they heard for themselves (4:42). Soon after, Jesus laments that the Jewish people will not believe without visible signs and wonders (4:48).

Over the next two chapters (5:20, 28; 6:14, 26, 30), the relationship between miraculous signs, belief and disbelief is reinforced. Many believe because of the signs; others—particularly the leaders—refuse to believe. Many also leave Jesus because they are baffled by Jesus' hard sayings (6:52, 60, 66). Again, Jesus must have been fully aware of how offensive the imagery of eating his flesh and drinking his blood was—to almost anyone, let alone a Jewish audience with its Mosaic proscription of tasting blood and human flesh. Yet, despite the opportunity to soften or clarify his statements, the author presents Jesus as leaving his listeners in chaos. Only after the resurrection do his words make sense.

John 7 and 8 cover a series of public conversations in which Jesus manages to mystify everyone, offend many and win over others. He leaves his audiences confused as to who he is, despite his repeated assertions as to his identity. Again, these are passages that make more sense after the resurrection, but are baffling at the time (for example, 7:1–10, 33–36; 8:27, 28).

Jesus' healing of the blind man in chapter 9 leads to yet more misunderstandings. The disciples misunderstand the reason for the man's blindness; the Jews misunderstand Jesus. Jesus asserts that the purpose of the blindness is to reveal the glory of God—the very purpose of prophecy and revelation. But in characteristically ironic style, only the blind man sees.

Then Jesus uses the figure of speech of the Good Shepherd that contains the prediction of his death and resurrection—but his audience fails to understand. In 10:24, 25, the Jews ask, "How long will you keep us in suspense? If you are the Messiah, tell us plainly." Jesus answers, "I have told you, and you do not believe. The works that I do in my Father's name testify to me." He adds that only his sheep can understand his voice, suggesting that the audience who can understand divine revelation is frequently limited. Finally, he appeals to them to believe on the basis of accomplished fact: "If I am not doing the works of my Father, then do not believe me. But if I do them, even though you do not believe me, believe the works, so that you may know and understand that the Father is in me and I am in the Father" (10:37, 38).

Jesus at first speaks in riddles concerning Lazarus' death, leading the disciples to think Lazarus is recovering (11:11–13). The author explains what Jesus means before having Jesus plainly state that Lazarus is dead. He adds, "For your sake I am glad I was not there, so that you may believe" (11:14, 15). In his tomb-side prayer, Jesus prays out loud: "I have said this for the sake of the crowd standing here, so that they may believe that you sent me" (11:42). The resurrection of Lazarus leads many to believe in him (11:45). Again, mystery and riddle only make sense after the event, leading to faith in Christ.

John the Evangelist explains the full significance of the unintentional prophecy of Caiaphas that it is better that one man dies for the people, but again this is only in hindsight that John is able to elucidate by writing long after the event (11:49–52). Similarly, the disciples don't understand the triumphal entry until after Jesus' glorification, when the significance of Zechariah 9:9

> Again, mystery and riddle only make sense after the event, leading to faith in Christ.

dawns on them (12:16). When a voice speaks from heaven confirming the glorification of Jesus, the crowd fails to understand, yet Jesus explains that it was for their benefit, then adds a prophecy of his death (12:28–33). None of these fully make sense until after the resurrection. Even the unbelief of the Jews is a fulfilment of prophecy (12:37–40) but one that takes hindsight to identify.

Jesus' final ironies

At the Passover supper, the disciples fail to understand Jesus' repeated pointers to the betrayal by Judas, their own desertion of him and Peter's triple denial (13:28), all of which again are plain after the event. While the disciples continue to fail to understand Jesus' final revelations, he promises them the Counsellor, and leaves them his peace—a peace that does not come from understanding his prophetic statements. No, it is a peace that comes from the presence of Jesus and of the Holy Spirit (14:5, 8, 25–27). The Holy Spirit will remind them of Jesus' words at the appropriate moment. The rest of Jesus' speech and prayer (chapters 15–17) again indicate his foreknowledge, and that the safety and prosperity of his followers lies in his love and the Father's love, made present through the Spirit.

In his final discourse at the Passover, Jesus speaks at length to prepare the disciples for his crucifixion, resurrection, ascension and the coming of the Holy Spirit, but does so largely in metaphoric language. Some disciples respond with, "What does he mean by this 'a little while'? We do not know what he is talking about" (16:18). Jesus adds a couple more metaphors before finally saying, "I have said these things to you in figures of speech. The hour is coming when I will no longer speak to you in figures, but will tell you plainly of the Father" (16:25). Relieved, his disciples exclaim, "Yes, now you are speaking plainly, not in any figure of speech! Now we know that you know all things, and do not need to have anyone question you; by this we believe that you came from God" (16:29, 30). Ironically, Jesus' exposition of the immediate future leaves his closest followers confused. Even when they claim to understand, their response to the events of the crucifixion and resurrection reveals that in fact they have not understood.

The trial, crucifixion and resurrection of Jesus are related in passages studded with prophetic fulfilment. Faith stems from people witnessing the fulfilment, although full understanding does not always follow (19:35–37). Peter and John see the empty tomb and believe, but still don't understand (20:3–9). Thomas refuses to believe until he literally sees (20:24–29). John concludes this chapter with, "Now Jesus did many other signs in the presence of his disciples, which are not written in this book. But these are written so that you may come to believe that Jesus is the Messiah, the Son of God, and that through believing you may have life in his name" (20:30, 31).

We can see that the gospel of John is rich in mysterious and enigmatic revelations of Jesus through "signs"—his words and actions—most of which only make sense after the event. Consistently, the purpose of these revelations is stated to be that of building faith in Jesus, the centrepiece of the revelation of God, rather than in letting us know the future. This gospel is not the only one to make such a point. The other gospels also note from time to time the mystery of Jesus and observe that the final understanding of revelation occurs after the crucifixion (for example, Matthew 16:1–12; Mark 9:31, 32; Luke 2:49,50; 9:43–45).

Revelation ironies

After noting these many examples of irony in this gospel, it struck me that there are strong similarities between the gospel and biblical apocalyptic texts.[4] Irony is a key device in the gospel of John, and also in scripture's last book, the Apocalypse, one of the Bible's most difficult books. Yet, ironically, it is called "Revelation." Both John and apocalyptic texts such as Daniel and Revelation have expert explanations—or glosses: explanatory notes written in the margin of a text or sometimes even in the text itself—often from heavenly beings (Jesus or angels), but ironically these don't necessarily lead to enlightenment at the time, as we have seen in the gospel of John.

The other gospels also note from time to time the mystery of Jesus and observe that the final understanding of revelation occurs after the crucifixion.

Daniel notes that despite Gabriel's elucidation, the vision of Daniel 8 left him "overcome" and "sick." He is "dismayed by the vision" and "did not understand it" (Daniel 8:27). Gabriel's further efforts to give Daniel understanding of the vision (9:23–27 and 10:12–12:4) are equally opaque, full of more highly detailed elaborations in figurative language that simultaneously offer some clarity and further mysteries.

Some of the glosses on the text of Revelation, often but not exclusively given by a heavenly being, are of a similar order (for example, Revelation 7:13–17; 13:18; 17:7–18). To pile irony on irony, the term "gloss" itself can not only mean an explanation of a difficult word or text, but also a misleading or deceptive interpretation. Given the difficulty in understanding apocalyptic texts, one must include the possibility that even these supposed explanations are deliberately obscure—at least to most readers or to most ages—despite any claims to being a "revelation."

God knows

For me, therefore, the gospel of John points the way to recognising that perhaps all prophetic texts present themselves not so much as a foretelling of future events, but as a revelation primarily about Jesus— as the opening line of Revelation confirms: "The revelation of [that is, both from and about] Jesus Christ." It suggests that a key purpose of prophetic revelation is not to forewarn God's people, but to assure them that God knows. For me, instead of building confidence through my ability to construct elaborate time-charts about end-times, prophecy asks that we lose self-trust and place it in the One who knows. It also suggests that prophecies that I still do not understand may not yet have been fulfilled.

Hindsight allows Jesus' followers to know that he understands the future and has it under control. Therefore, we can trust him for what is yet to come. This does not exclude other approaches to prophecy, including its potential to alert us to the future. The Jewish leaders in Herod's day understood prophecy sufficiently to know that the Messiah would be born in Bethlehem (see Matthew 2:4–6). However, a considerable amount of prophecy still remained obscure. Matthew added a little note of alert to his readers in Jesus' apocalyptic discourse (Matthew 24:15), which told them that the meaning of Jesus' statement could only fully make sense later, since it was addressed to later readers rather than to Jesus' immediate audience.

So my attempt to understand the enigma of Jesus in the gospel of John, expressed through riddles and irony, has led me to discover a bigger picture: that all revelation—the entire Bible, in effect—is designed to point to God, rather than to mere information, time sequences of events or anything else so petty. Its deliberate imprecisions are intended to save us from the presumptions of self-assurance, shifting the focus from our supposed wisdom to the omniscience of God. In the words of Jesus, it is given to us to bring us peace and freedom from fear. Its purpose is that as prophetic words are fulfilled, we may say, "Now we are sure that Jesus is the one, for he warned us of this. He knows the future and so we have his peace."

THE ENIGMA OF JESUS IN THE GOSPEL OF JOHN

1. R Alan Culpepper, *Anatomy of the Fourth Gospel*, Philadelphia, PA: Fortress Press, 1983, pages 165–6.

2. Such as Warren Carter, *John: Storyteller, Interpreter, Evangelist*, Peabody MA: Hendrickson, 2006, and Gail O'Day, *Revelation in the Fourth Gospel: Narrative mode and theological claim*, Philadelphia PA: Fortress Press, 1986.

3. Paul D Duke, *Irony in the Fourth Gospel*, Atlanta, GA: John Knox Press, 1985, has written an entire book on the ironies found in John's gospel.

4. This idea is not original: scholars such as John Ashton (*Understanding the Fourth Gospel*, Oxford: Clarendon Press, 1993), John Painter (*The Quest for the Messiah: the history, literature and theology of the Johannine community* (2nd edition), Nashville: Abingdon, 1993) and J L Martyn (*History and Theology in the Fourth Gospel* (2nd edition), Nashville: Abingdon, 1979), have elaborated the connection between John and apocalyptic texts.

The Samaritan "Other" in The Gospel of John

Jane Fernandez

My fascination with the Gospel of John began as a child framed around my mother's faith and drawn from the imprints of the drama of the cross and resurrection of Christ, as it unfolded through various stages of my childhood. Looking back, I think being raised largely by my widowed mother accounts for my being drawn to the scene where Jesus gives his mother to the "disciple whom he loved" (see John 19:26, 27). The compassion and generosity flowing out of that gesture had a deep resonance for me because I grew up largely in the shadow of my mother's sense of abandonment and helplessness.

Even today, the overpowering sense of intimacy emanating from John's gospel, centred in that profound exchange before the cross, continues to be an abiding presence and guiding light informing my own faith in the personal crises I have encountered. There are several other soft images of Christ that John testifies to, especially evident in his account of the miracles and—of particular interest to our discussion in this chapter—the Samaritan narrative of John 4. But standing in sharp contrast to these soft images are strikingly harsh scenes in which Christ seems unrelenting in his judgement and criticism, including—for example—the controversial "children of the devil" episode (see 8:44). Clearly, the Gospel of John invites us to deal with these tensions.

Several scholars note that John appears to be writing for a "spectrum of readers" outside the Jewish enclave. The nature of this intended readership suggests a widening of the borders of the Jewish world, highlighted by Jesus' interrogation of Jewish thought and practice. Set against a Greco-Roman background, John's gospel appears to conscientiously transcend the social and religious formations of his time. If John's gospel is inclusive, it appears to focus on constructing a theology for an audience beyond the confines of the Jewish world.[1]

Scenes such as the temple confrontation and Jesus' encounters with the Pharisees reflect Jesus' frustrations with a community inbred and in crisis, set against His looming death. The pace and intensity of John's gospel reflect its urgency to mount a gospel for the world. This is emphasised by the interrogative tone of John's gospel, and the several ruptures of action and disruptions of meaning within the text, all of which come together to challenge the seeming coherence of the laws and social practices of the Jews. My interest is in extracting for study one dimension of these ruptures or contradictions, seen in Jesus' attempts to breach the deeply ingrained prejudices of the Jews against the Samaritans.

Reading frame

My reading of the Gospel of John is drawn from literary, rather than biblical or theological studies, so my reading is exploratory and text-based. Further, my reading is influenced by my postcolonial background and as such, I come to the Gospel of John with a deep appreciation of it as a selective "biographical account" of Jesus' life. I remind myself that the gaps and omissions in the account caution against overstating the "literality" of each Scriptural verse.[2] This caution is important, given the powerful resonance of the "Word" and the "centrality of the journey motif in the narration of Jesus' life."[3] Against the backdrop of the "Word" made flesh, God's transcendence hovers over our limited understandings, even as John's gospel propels us forward through the journey motif to greater self-awareness.

I have set out in this chapter to demonstrate how John's gospel negates debates about the insider/outsider status of "the chosen" to focus instead on the identity of Christ as the "Chosen One." Both the Jewish idea of "Israel" and the Christian community's identity as "the new Israel" cause divisions between people. The claims of both Jews and Christians to exclusive election contradicts the inclusivity of John's gospel.

John's gospel opens on the authority of the *Logos*, Christ as the "Word" who was "with God in the beginning," and through whom "all things were made." In that Word "was life, and the life was the light of *all* people" (1:1–4, emphasis mine). The *Logos* marks the ascendancy of Christ as Son of God from the beginning of time. The elements of the flesh and spirit, of material and poetic power, of language and the senses, are all encapsulated in the *Logos*—the "Word Incarnate." The Word establishes our human finiteness in contrast to God's infinity. As pastor and New Testament scholar Jaime Clark-Soles points out, "Jesus transforms the mundane into the spiritual by participating in the mundane."[4] The mystical opening, then, sets the parameters for our reading, pointing beyond the narrow confines of our limited knowing to search continually for something other, something irretrievably elusive. Our reading of John's gospel must continually reflect that expansiveness and generosity of the *Logos* as a gift encompassing all creation and all humanity. It is this generosity that I as a reader anticipate and find in John's gospel—and that invites us on a journey of inclusiveness.

My aim is to do a close study of the appeal to the Samaritan motif by threading John 4 and John 8 to lead us to the central trajectory of John's gospel: its broadening treatment of the "chosen" in terms of faith and belief. Ultimately, God and Christ belong to the world and the grace born through the death and resurrection of Christ is available to all who trust in Him: "There is no longer Jew or Greek, there is no longer slave or free, there is no longer male and female; for all of you are one in Christ Jesus" (Galatians 3.28).

Sacrificial violence

The lens I wish to appropriate for my reading of the Samaritan theme is René Girard's theory of scapegoating or sacrificial violence.[5] Girard argues that society since primitive times has rationalised its survival through the scapegoat mechanism. He argues that central to culture is the concept of the "alien" or the scapegoat who must be sought out and eliminated for the preservation of that culture.[6] The election of a scapegoat, derived from the tradition of the ancient *pharmakon*, suggests that the perpetuation of peace is ironically built on the framework of violence.[7] Girard asserts that the "violent unanimity principle"—the consensus around the appointment and election of the scapegoat—provides the community with the illusion of unity.[8] This violence is managed through a framework of myths, rituals and prohibitions.

Accordingly, Girard argues that peace is essentially bought at the terrible cost of violence sanctified through a system by which human beings consensually and ritualistically choose a scapegoat, through whom they purge their fears of violence. Girard argues that the ritualisation of this scapegoat mechanism has become so embedded in the psyche of human society that it has become the *modus operandi* of our existence. Girard asserts that the survival of ritual violence is built on its being characterised as "good" or "holy" violence and the premise of its seeming generative value to the community.[9] This "wilful misunderstanding" of the need for violence to maintain peace has survived even into our so-called enlightened times through the theological basis for sacrifice. Accordingly Girard argues that in this sense "violence is sacred":

> The *sacred is violence*, but if religious man worships violence it is only insofar as the worship of violence is supposed to bring peace; religion is entirely concerned with peace, but the means it has of bringing it about are never free of sacrificial violence.[10]

What we have, then, is a perverse system through which the "cure for violence is sought through violence."[11] Girard argues that it is Christ who puts an end to this vicious cycle by absorbing the scapegoat mechanism into His body. The death of God in the person of Christ breaks the sacrificial mechanism and calls for an end to all scapegoating.[12]

My purpose is to employ Girard in studying the framework of the scapegoating of Samaritans as treated in John's Gospel. I intend to drill down through the narrative to the embedded mysteries, employing if you like, a "hermeneutics of suspicion" to disrupt the seeming neatness of the surface narrative.[13] To be able to do that, I begin from the premise that the surface-level narrative leaves the question of Samaritan "guilt" uncontested until Christ exposes the scapegoating mechanism in John 4 through His exchange with the Samaritan woman.

The Samaritan "Other"

John 4 is pivotal in establishing a way out of the circuits of ritual violence against marginalised groups—in this case, the Samaritans. If we tried to trace the history of the persecution of the Samaritans, we would find ourselves on a slippery slope, given the complex historical and social overlays of Jewish–Samaritan dealings. However, in Girardian terms, the guilt or innocence of the victim is irrelevant to scapegoating. All scapegoating is sustained through a wilful delusion or through the "nonconscious" character of scapegoating. This "nonconscious element" protects "scapegoaters" from the truth of the violence they represent.[14] These delusions are fortified instead by a system built often on religious rules and defended by tradition and practice. The potent power of scapegoating as in the case of the Samaritans is in the group defence of its position on the basis of theology, meaning that their persecution is couched in religious terms. Hence the practice of persecution is deemed "respectable."

Accordingly, a common rationale for the marginalisation of the Samaritans was their supposed irreverence or untouchability. They were:

> painted as mongrels or half-breeds due to intermarriage with non-Israelite groups after the Assyrian invasion of 722–721 BCE. Their priesthood and sanctuary were judged illegitimate, their text of the Torah corrupt, and their cult syncretistic—contaminated by the paganism of their Mesopotamian conquerors.[15]

The branding of the Samaritans in terms of their hybridity, their allegedly corrupt sacred texts, and their contaminating influence on

Jewish life and practice set them up as classic scapegoats. In reality, Jews and Samaritans had more commonalities than differences, and if anything, the Samaritans were more conservative:

> The Samaritans worshipped YHWH as the one true God, but revered Mt Gerizim rather than Mt Zion as their holy place, thought their line of Levitical priests to be legitimate (as opposed to that of the Jerusalem temple), and accepted only the Torah and not the prophets (*nebim*) or the "writings" (*ketubim*) as their sacred Scripture. . . . Significantly, historical evidence debunks the idea that Samaritans' religion was any more syncretistic than that of their cousins who worshipped in Jerusalem: quite the contrary, it was a more conservative expression of Israelite religion, far less open to changes.[16]

While Jewish prejudice against Samaritans is treated at length in John 4 through the Samaritan woman narrative, the key moment awaits us in John 8 where, ironically, Christ himself is charged with being a "Samaritan and demon possessed" (8:48). Like all scapegoating, the scapegoating of the Samaritans, by necessity, over-extends itself in John 8:48 when the angst against Samaritans is transferred to Jesus. The fact that Jesus provokes this transference in John 8::44 is particularly enlightening in that Jesus forces into the open the politics of exclusivity that Jews thrived upon, foreshadowing the role he will play as scapegoat for Jewish—as well as the world's—ignorance.

Jesus and "the Jews"

It would appear that some attention needs to be paid to this exchange between Jesus and this group of Jews in John 8. Undoubtedly, Jesus' characterisation of this specific group of Jews in John 8:48 as "children of the devil" is not intended to vilify all Jews. Such positions taken by various groups have no basis in John 8. Regrettably, the "children of the devil" verses have been exploited by many—including the early and Reformation church—to brand Jews as "Christ-killers." Siker argues that "history has demonstrated . . . the use of these texts (so-called proof-texts) in legitimating acts of horror against a people." She asserts:

From the damning preaching of Melito in the second century to the equally vicious condemnations of Martin Luther in the 16th century to the unspeakable horrors of the Nazi regime, the gospels have fuelled the fires of prejudice and outrage against the Jews, and Christianity has been accused of being anti-Semitic in origin.[17]

She also cites Rosemary Radford Ruether who argues that not only is the "origin of anti-Semitism most properly placed at the door of nascent Christianity, but . . . that it is an inherent and inextricable part of Christianity."[18]

The grand irony missed by those who hold this position is their denial of the context for this exchange. To begin with, Jesus was speaking to his own people and the strong overtones suggest a degree of familiarity in such exchanges between Jesus and groups of Jews. The interpretation of these verses as anti-Semitic gloss over the inherent internal contradiction in that Christ was himself a Jew.[19]

The expression "Jew/Jews" is often times a negative term. It may describe individuals, the people, or the leadership of the Jewish nation. Jews are oftentimes portrayed as being in opposition to Jesus and not believing in him. However, there are important exceptions. Jesus is a Jew. Salvation comes from the Jews and there are Jews who believe in Jesus and follow him. . . . Nowhere do we find a wholesale condemnation of all Jews of all times. Salvation comes from the Jews through Jesus Christ and is extended to both Jews and Gentiles.[20]

Clearly, a symbolic reading of Jesus' words is in order. We cannot ignore the emotive overflow in Jesus' stance. Flowing out of His frustrations, we see a very human Jesus! Judging from Jesus' sense of fatigue, it would appear these arguments with different groups of Jews were not necessarily new. More importantly, John reminds us that these were believers—Jews "who had believed in Him" (8:31). To them, Jesus dictates a clear and outright challenge, commissioning freedom through true discipleship and locating this in the question of trust.

The ensuing dialogue between Jesus and the groups of Jews run in two polarised strands: the Jews fixating on their Abrahamic genealogy and Christ contesting their over-reliance on their birthright, as well as their self-righteousness. These verses appear to complicate the issue of identity through the Abraham discourse. What Christ attempts to do is to shift the question of paternity to the spiritual realm, to questions of faith and action: *to believe, to hear, to trust.* How to belong to God or to Satan becomes then a matter of informed belief. As the following verses demonstrate, birthright does not preclude us from individual spiritual responsibility. Note the trajectory of the verses, beginning with (1) a circular agreement between Jesus and the Jews about their Abrahamic genealogy, (2) Jesus' exposing Jewish contradictions of their Abraham-inherited character and (3) closing on the premise that love for God's Son is the only legitimate kinship.

1. "We are descendants of Abraham" (8:33).
   "I know that you are descendants of Abraham" (8:37).
   "Abraham is our father" (8.39a).

2. "Jesus said to them, 'If you were Abraham's children, you would be doing what Abraham did, but now you are trying to kill me, a man who has told you the truth that I heard from God. This is not what Abraham did. You are indeed doing what your father does'" (8:39b–41a).

3. "They said to him, 'We are not illegitimate children; we have one father, God himself'" (8:41b).
   "Jesus said to them, 'If God were your Father, you would love me'" (8:42).

I contend that Jesus was outlining that the Abrahamic tradition is aligned to faith in God, not the reverse! The irony of Jesus' words cannot be missed. Being descendants of Abraham and sons of God, you should know better! By not acting accordingly, you by default choose to belong to "your father, the devil" (8:44). Jesus' words here are no harsher than elsewhere in the gospels when he speaks about the fruits of sin. The Jews, by their closed-mindedness, are a proxy for all of us, in our moments of denial, distrust and faithlessness. We are all open to the same charge. Christ makes clear that the way of God is truth while the way of Satan is falsehood. The choice to belong to God opens up our senses: "Whoever is from God hears the words of God. The reason you do not hear them is that you are not from God" (8:47).

Girard's counsel is helpful here, arguing that Jesus' rather brutal summations mark the urgency with which he "intervenes . . . at the point when everything is ready to slide into a limitless violence."[21] This urgency is explicit in John 8:43–46:

> Why do you not understand what I say? It is because you cannot accept my word. You are from your father the devil, and you choose to do your father's desires. He was a murderer from the beginning and does not stand in the truth, because there is no truth in him. When he lies, he speaks according to his own nature, for he is a liar and the father of lies. But because I tell the truth, you do not believe me. Which of you convicts me of sin? If I tell the truth, why do you not believe me?

The passage appears to allude to the obstinancy of this group of Jews. What is it that Jesus was trying to teach that was so difficult for them to hear? Was it about his Sonship? Was it about their Pharisaic attitudes? Was it about their self-righteousness? Was it about their attitude to Gentiles? Was it about sectarianism? The key to answering this comes to us in the Jews' charge against Jesus: "Are we not right in saying that you are a Samaritan and have a demon?" (8:48). How did the Samaritan label interject into this exchange? I suggest that "Samaritan" is a catch-all for Jewish animosity and angst, essentially a scapegoat. In this light, Jesus' confrontational stance becomes clear. It is aimed at breaking through layers of ingrained Jewish prejudices and Jewish notions of entitlement.

Jesus the Samaritan

The *samaritanising* of Jesus by the Jews has several implications. I want to consider this through exploring the structure of John 8, with specific attention to the adulteress narrative.[22] John 8:12–47 is sandwiched between the adulteress narrative sequence and the charge in John 8:48 that Jesus is "a Samaritan and demon-possessed." Between Jesus' exposé in John 8:11—"Neither do I condemn you"—and John 8:48 is a series of exchanges between Jesus and the Pharisees on the identity and authority of Jesus. Two competing discourses emerge, namely the divine authority of Christ in John's gospel pitted against the distorted perceptions of Jewish authority.

Accordingly, the verses oscillate between Jesus' claims to His Father's authority and the Jews' challenge of His authority. This heated exchange is juxtaposed against the silence and tranquillity of the scene with the adulteress. The soft image of Jesus silent, bent over, inscribing in sand forgiveness for the adulteress prefaces the rest of the more animated and fiery exchanges. Read in the context of Jesus' inclusiveness and compassion, the "children of the devil" charge reflects how Jesus' anger is manifest on behalf of the dispossessed and the marginalised. This *samaritanising* of Jesus is ironically the most powerful antidote to Jewish prejudice. Aimed at reversing Jesus' insider status to an outsider status, it collapses those assumed hierarchies for us as readers.

Poetically, Jesus' absorption of this role makes Him a double to the Samaritans, redeeming the Samaritans from their outsider status and destabilising for readers centuries of prejudice against Samaritans. What accrues further credibility for John 8:48 is that it becomes a structural hook, linking John 8 to John 4. What is obvious is that the reference to "Samaritans" in John 8 evokes the figure of the Samaritan woman in John 4. By the time Jesus is cast as a Samaritan, he has already redeemed the Samaritan reputation through his encounter with the Samaritan woman at the well. The irony of labelling–mislabelling–relabelling is not lost on us as we are faced with a fresh understanding of the plurality of our own identities. Ironically, the Jews' charge—"You are a Samaritan"—juxtaposes the Samaritan woman's "You are a Jew, I am a Samaritan" (see 4:9), highlighting the group politics of the former and the internalised *Othering* of the latter.

Rewriting the Samaritan status

In John 4, this phenomenon of *Othering* is raised through the Samaritan woman's self-declaration of her *Other* status, emphasised in the bracketed aside by John. In response to Jesus' request for a drink, the Samaritan woman declares without hesitation, "'How is it that you, a Jew, ask a drink of me, a woman of Samaria?' (Jews do not share things in common with Samaritans.)" (4:9). The Samaritan woman signals her identity in terms of her polarised status in respect to Jews/Samaritans. Through her question, she articulates her dispossessed status, as well as charts the long and suppressed history of oppression and victimisation suffered by her people. It is particularly significant that John's gospel uses the Samaritan woman as a mouthpiece for the Samaritan predicament, because her humiliation and ritualised oppression was well-known: "Samaritan women [were] stereotyped as 'menstruants from the cradle' and hence perpetually unclean [as established by the laws of] Leviticus 15:19."[23]

Against this backdrop, Jesus' easy dialogue enables the woman to break through the social taboos she has been subject to. Boers notes appropriately that Jesus creates "an atmosphere in which the woman feels comfortable enough to raise the right issues for Jesus to respond to, . . . [that is] the religious and social issues which separate *Ioudaioi* and Samaritans."[24] By doing so, Jesus sets the tone and scope for generational change evidenced by the Samaritan woman's subsequent appeal to their common ancestry, through the allusions to Joseph and Jacob:

> [H]er reference to Jacob as "our father" can be understood on two levels: if "our" refers to Samaritans, then it stands as an affirmation of their ancestral link to the patriarchs, but if it refers to Jesus and the woman, then it serves as an opportune reminder of the ancient common origin shared by all the descendants of Israel.[25]

The Samaritan woman serves a double function: she fulfils the archetype of the scapegoat and stands also as a symbol for the collective marginalisation of the Samaritan community. Fundamentally, she carries a double-economy of the burden of marginalisation. In terms of the scapegoat theory, we could argue that the gospel's employment of a woman serves to increase the "mythical guilt" of the Samaritan scapegoat. Her double-marginalisation brings to the centre of John's gospel two strands of prejudice for scrutiny: the prejudice against Samaritans and the prejudice against women. The encounter between Jesus and the Samaritan woman raises the issue of collective sectarian prejudice, while almost immediately elevating and prioritising the profile of women's dispossession. The choise of Jacob's Well for this encounter is worth exploring.

Significance of Jacob's Well

Jesus meeting the Samaritan woman at the site of Jacob's Well is not incidental to our argument. Jacob's Well generates an imaginative and psychological connection to the past. The place raises the trace of memory leading back to the stories of Jacob and Joseph, challenging myths of difference and notions of purity, through establishing the common ancestry of Jew and Samaritan and deflating all impure connotations through the memory of slavery and exile retrieved through the history of Joseph. The well could be regarded as a repository of witness and testimony, attesting to the generations of lives of people from both sides of the divide who had been nourished, physically and spiritually, by the same patriarchs and from the same gospel. In this sense, the well holds the histories, stories, love, pain, sorrows, fears and hopes of not just the people of Samaria but all travellers. It provides a labyrinth, a threshold, enabling multiple crossings. By choosing to rest at Jacob's Well, Jesus superimposes the historical traces we have just discussed by substituting Jacob's Well with his body, the new labyrinth for the world.

The allusions to water are not incidental either as we will see in the "Living Water" discourse. The dialogue that follows between the Samaritan woman and Jesus demonstrates how Jesus enables the Samaritan woman to negotiate the path from victim to free status through him. As Girardian theory establishes, the only way the scapegoating can be broken is through the victim's baulking against the system. Jesus identifies with the victim and baulks against a system that had displaced Samaritans for centuries by enabling the woman's speech.

The "Living Water" discourse

While John 4 demonstrates Jesus' passion for the world, it also demonstrates how personal the journey of salvation is to Jesus. The encounter at Jacob's Well is at best an intimate encounter between human frailty and divine wisdom. Given her alienation and dispossession, the Samaritan woman has no empirical substance to draw upon to find her own voice. Jesus gives her the cue to speak! He enables her voice by "initiating a dialogue."[26] And this Jesus does by way of a question, which on the surface suggests nothing more than a need for Jesus to satisfy his own physiological need but the allusion to water cannot be missed. On the surface level, Jesus is thirsty and needs a drink. But in asking a Samaritan woman for drink, Jesus risks breaking the taboos established from the fear of contamination, a predicament of which the Samaritan woman is clearly aware. "By asking her for a drink, Jesus breaks through a very concrete and personal expression of prejudice: *Ioudaioi* believed they incurred ritual defilement by contact with food, drink or anything handled by a Samaritan."[27]

Given this taboo, Jesus' actions appear to intentionally subvert Jewish laws. The result is that he empowers the woman by extricating and exposing the embedded prejudice against Samaritans. If the depth of Jacob's Well alludes to the immeasurable capacity for prejudice in the light of Jewish history, the well's association to "water" also provides the antidote to prejudice through the allusions to cleansing and renewal.

In this light, the "Living Water" discourse through which Jesus provides the Samaritan woman with spiritual nourishment Is instructional.

> "Everyone who drinks this water will be thirsty again, but whoever drinks the water I give him will never thirst. Indeed, the water I give him will become in him a spring of water welling up to eternal life." The woman said to him, "Sir, give me this water so that I won't get thirsty and have to keep coming here to draw water" (4:13–15).

By comparing the materiality of water to that of his embodiment of eternal Living Water, Jesus levels the playing field between Jews and Samaritans offering the latter with the same "gift" available to the former. Through His selection of the Samaritan woman as heir to eternal life, Jesus breaches all the rules of scapegoating, collapsing all hierarchies through prophesying that "the hour is coming, and is now here, when the true worshippers will worship the Father in spirit and truth" (4:23), thereby substituting all places of worship with his body.

The end of scapegoating

John's gospel powerfully portrays Christ's ethics of love as an antidote to ritualised violence. Christ comes to put an end to scapegoating. Christ's willingness as God to submit to death on the cross calls for an end to the ritual of scapegoating. What Christ's death demonstrates is the vulnerability of the scapegoat mechanism in that it eventually exceeds the limits of its own boundaries, through the loss of distinctions between sanctioned and unsanctioned violence. The crucifixion registers this loss of distinctions in demanding the death of a God. Christ names the unspeakable at the heart of society, by demonstrating how close to home the question of violence and the violation of the *Other* is, even as close as the religious and sacred texts we cherish.[28] We are reminded of the responsibility we must each accept for interpreting the Scriptures so that our interpretations contribute to unity and community-building, reflecting Christ's gospel of love and peace.

1. C R Koester, *The Word of Life: A Theology of John's Gospel*, Grand Rapids, MI: Williams B Eerdmans, 2008, page 6.

2. F F Segovia, "The Gospel of John" in Fernando F Segovia and R S Sugirtharajah (editors), *A Postcolonial Commentary on the New Testament Writings*, T and T Clark, 2009, page 174.

3. ibid.

4. Jaime Clark-Soles, "I will Raise [Whom?] Up on the Last Day: Anthropology as a Feature of Johannine Eschatology" in Francisco Lozada Jr & Tom Thatcher (editors), *New Currents Through John: A Global Perspective*, Atlanta, GA: Society of Biblical Literature, 2006, pages 37–8.

5. R Girard, *Violence and the Sacred* (translated Patrick Gregory), Baltimore, MD: Johns Hopkins University Press, 1979.

6. ibid.

7. W Burkert, René Girard, & Jonathan Z Smith, *Violent Origins: Ritual Killing and Cultural Formation*, Stanford, CA: Stanford University Press, 1997, pages 73–4. See also R Girard, *Things Hidden Since the Foundation of the World*, Stanford, CA: Stanford University Press, 1987, page 131.

8. Girard, *Violence and the Sacred*, op cit, page 12.

9. See both *Violence and the Sacred* and *Things Hidden Since the Foundation of the World*.

10. Girard, *Things Hidden Since the Foundation of the World*, op cit, page 32.

11. ibid.

12. See Girard, *Things Hidden Since the Foundation of the World*, op cit.

13. See S Bigger, "Book Review: Ricoeur and the Hermeneutics of Suspicion," *Journal of Beliefs*

& *Values: Studies in Religion & Education*, Routledge, May 2011. Bigger cites Ricoeur's premise for "the need for suspicion so that our understanding and knowledge are not subject to other people's honest or dishonest persuasiveness."

14. Burkert, Girard & Smith, op cit, pages 73–5.

15. E J Wyckoff, "Jesus in Samaria (John 4:4–42): A Model for Cross-Cultural Ministry," *Biblical Theology Bulletin: A Journal of Bible and Theology*, Sage, 2005, page 90.

16. ibid, citing Meier, pages 534, 542.

17. J Y Siker, "Anti-Judaism in the Gospels According to Matthew, Mark, Luke, John, and Mel," *Pastoral Psychology*, vol 53 no 4, March 2005, page 307.

18. Cited in Siker, ibid, page 308.

19. Koester, op cit, page 76. See also Ekkehardt Müller, "The Jews and the Messianic Community in Johannine Literature," *DavarLogos*, vol 4 no 2, 2005, page 170, for summary of positive treatment of Jews.

20. Müller, op cit, pages 175–80.

21. Girard, *Things Hidden Since the Foundation of the World*, op cit, page 207.

22. Some would argue that my premise here is faulty given its intertextual implications since biblical scholars believe the adulteress narrative is a later addition to John's gospel. However, this is not relevant to my purpose as a literary reader. In the first instance, my reading is a formalist-based literary reading of John's gospel, as I know it. The text is paramount and authorial intentions become secondary. Second, I read John's gospel in its final form and as it is presented to me as a reader of the 21st century. So, if we were to consider how John 8:48 is framed within the chapter, we would have to ask why the story of the adulteress prefaces the rest of the chapter.

23. Daube cited in Wyckoff, op cit, page 92.

24. Boers cited in Wyckoff, op cit, page 92.

25. Wyckoff, op cit, page 93.

26. ibid, page 92.

27. Daube cited in Wyckoff, op cit, page 92.

28. See Girard in *Violence and the Sacred* and *Things Hidden Since the Foundation of the World*, op cit, on sacrificial excess and Christ's role in breaking the circuits of violence.

The God Who Stoops

Nathan Brown

Washing another person's feet is one of the most profound symbols and memorials of the Christian faith. It is observed occasionally in various Christian traditions, although rarely or not at all in some. Having grown up in Adventist churches in which I have regularly washed the already-clean feet of family, friends and occasionally strangers, it is perhaps not as shocking to me as it should be. Culturally and practically, it can seem a long way from the dusty feet and dim upper room to the bathed and polished Sabbath best in a contemporary church's back room.

But by physically bowing, an appropriate attitude and imaginative engagement, it should be no less profound to re-enact this act of humility today—as Jesus said. It is a pattern for how we should put our faith into practice between the times when we might do it literally in a church or worship setting—as Jesus did. As disciples of the God who stooped, Christian believers should be people who stoop in service to their fellow human beings, particularly to those in need.

In this sense, Jesus was the first and greatest to stoop—and to set this profound example of attitude and action: "Now before the festival of the Passover, Jesus knew that his hour had come to depart from this world and go to the Father. Having loved his own who were in the world, he loved them to the end" (John 13:1). Another Bible translation makes it more explicit, that on this night and in this act, "he showed them the full extent of his love."[1]

Throughout the Johannine writings—the gospel and apostolic letters—the love of God is a constant theme, so it is interesting to note what he regarded as the crescendo of this refrain. This was the moment that showed the "full extent" of that love. John then proceeds to describe Jesus, the eternal Son of God, washing the feet of His dusty and doubting disciples, one by one. According to John, this was the greatest, most profound expression of the love of God—demonstrated in an act of incredible humility and service.

Reading the stories

As a student of stories and storytelling—both academically and professionally—I am fascinated by how Bible stories that we often consider in isolation fit together, echo each other and can offer different or deeper readings. Narrative readings of the Bible—a collection of stories and histories, among other literary forms—can offer some different perspectives from those of theological or textual readings.

Considering the stories that set the scene for that of Jesus stooping to wash His disciples' feet—a story that is unique to John's gospel—one feature to notice is that this is the third chapter that begins with reference to a similar posture in anointing, washing and drying feet. While the numbered chapters are a later addition to the gospel text, the unfolding narrative links the episodes (see John 11:2; 12:3; 13:3).

The reference at the beginning of Chapter 11 is brief but gives one verse to introduce Mary, a sister of Lazarus, as "the one who anointed the Lord with perfume and wiped his feet with her hair" (John 11:2). The action moves on but not before we should pause to reflect that it is unusual to introduce a character in the story by something they have not yet done, an action that has not yet taken place. So this profound act of love and service has been foreshadowed as something significant that is about to happen.

But it is not until the opening verses of Chapter 12—beginning the story of Jesus' final week of ministry—that the storyteller expands on this introduction of Mary, narrating her anointing Jesus' feet in the midst of a dinner party. While there is an obvious element of pre-burial anointing recognised in Mary's act—which is an important element of the narrative momentum toward Jesus' crucifixion—the stooping posture of washing seems to point forward again to Jesus' action at the beginning of Chapter 13.

A borrowed idea?

In Matthew's and Mark's tellings of a similar story (see Matthew 26:6–13 and Mark 14:3–9), there is a promise that "wherever this good news is proclaimed in the whole world, what she has done will be told in remembrance of her" (Matthew 26:13). This prediction is certainly fulfilled in the inclusion of this story in the gospel accounts still being read and shared some 2000 years later. But perhaps the explicit statement did not need to be included in John's story because another of the ways in which her act would be remembered is that which begins the next episode of his story of Jesus. Perhaps the remembering of her act would be best inaugurated in Jesus' instruction—after washing His disciples' feet—to "do as I have done to you" (John 13:15). In following Jesus' example, we also follow Mary's example.

There is evidence to suggest that many congregations in the early Christian church practised footwashing as a spiritual ritual and an act of both remembrance and service.[2] While we have often explained Jesus' action as precipitated by the absence of a servant in the upper room on that Passover night, that the early believers took this aspect of Jesus' instructions literally suggests they perceived this as more intentional than we might have assumed.

There is no evidence in John's narrative that Jesus' action arose from an oversight by their hosts. Indeed, a reader could wonder if Mary's act a few days earlier might have planted an idea in Jesus' mind. As He had defended her from their criticism, Jesus might have devised one last plan to try to get through to the proud and stubborn disciples what His kingdom was truly about. As the disciples see Jesus stooping before each of them in turn, they would have been reminded of what Mary had done and how they had attacked the waste, the inappropriateness, the excess of her act of love. And now the One whose feet had been washed was washing their feet.

In so doing, Jesus "showed them the full extent of his love"—and the three instances of this "stooping" action in John 11, 12 and 13 position

Jesus' act as the climax of this sequence. What Mary did was considered scandalous; how much more this act of Jesus. In John's narrating of the story, he is careful to make clear what is taking place in this seemingly simple act.

Jesus — "God with us"

Immediately before John tells us about what Jesus did on that night, he pauses in the story to remind us of exactly who it was doing this: "Jesus, knowing that the Father had given all things into his hands, and that he had come from God and was going to God" (John 13:3). We will never understand the dramatic stooping action of God in becoming human in the person of Jesus (see John 1:1–14). The Creator of the universe became a creature. The unlimited Ruler of the universe became a human baby with all those physical limitations. What even all of that means is a profound mystery—but a wonderful and world-changing mystery.

We need to remember this reality whenever we hear the stories of Jesus. The most profound stories about Jesus are not the big crowds, the great stories and the public miracles but the time He spent with individual people—Nicodemus in a late-night conversation (see John 3), the woman at the well (see John 4), intimate conversations with people He healed (see, for example, John 9:35–39), conversations with Mary, Martha and Lazarus in their home (see John 11 and 12), the time and attention He gave to each of His disciples in different personalised ways (see John 13:36-38; 14:5-7; 14:8-9; 14:22-24), Mary in the garden on the morning of the resurrection (see John 20), cooking breakfast on the beach for a few of His disciples (see John 21). In each of these moments, we see the God of the universe interacting personally with one man or woman at a time, as if that person was all that mattered to Him in the whole universe. By so many standards, it was terribly inefficient, perhaps even risky and wasteful, but a remarkable insight into what God is like and the love He has for every one of us.

And this is the same Jesus who stoops to wash the disciples' feet one by one. A most personal act, as well as a powerful symbol—an enactment—of what "Word became flesh and lived among us" (John 1:14) was all about: demonstrating "the full extent of his love."

Stooping to wash those feet

Another aspect of the scene draws us to Jesus the great servant. Jesus knew what was going on in the dark background to that night: "The devil had already put it into the heart of Judas son of Simon Iscariot to betray him" (John 13:2). Jesus "knew who was to betray him" (verse 11) and where that would end for both Jesus and Judas. Within a few hours, their fates would be finalised.

It seems the meal was already in progress, but Jesus, the Son of God, got up from the table to perform an act of great humility and wonder. The picture of the God of the whole universe stooping to wash the feet of a group of ordinary men is amazing. Added to this wonder is the cultural stigma attached to footwashing in those days—it was the work of the lowest servants—and the fact that those feet that He washed included the feet of the one who was about to betray Him to His enemies and another who was going to deny knowing Him later that night.

The servanthood and humility of God is one of the most profound realities of the Christian faith.

The servanthood and humility of God is one of the most profound realities of the Christian faith. For those of us who have heard it many times, who have ceremonially washed clean church feet for much of our lives, we might too easily take it for granted. Yet it is a kind of love that transcends the best humanity can offer or even fully understand:

> The love for the less fortunate is a beautiful thing—the love for those who suffer, for those who are poor, the sick, the failures, the unlovely. This is compassion, and it touches the heart of the world. The love for the more fortunate is a rare thing—to love those who succeed where we fail, to rejoice without envy with those who rejoice, the love of the poor for the rich . . . The world is always bewildered by its saints. And then there is the love for the enemy—love for the one who does not love you but mocks, threatens and inflicts pain. The tortured's love for the torturer. This is God's love. It conquers the world.[3]

The ultimate stooping

We must never forget that this act of footwashing was the beginning of a 24-hour ordeal that ended with the tortured, crucified and dead Jesus being placed in a borrowed tomb as the sun set that Friday evening. In one sense, His stooping to wash the disciples' feet was the prelude to stooping lower still to lift the whole world toward resurrection and hope: "He goes down to come up again and to bring the whole ruined world up with Him. . . . He must stoop in order to lift, he must almost disappear under the load before he incredibly straightens his back and marches off with the whole mass swaying on his shoulders."[4]

The magnitude of the stoop is commensurate to the height from which it came. Sampling from various Old Testament passages to build the argument, the introduction to the Gospel of John is a poem to the absolute divinity of Jesus. At the beginning of the poem we read: "In the beginning was the Word, and the Word was with God, and the Word was God. He was in the beginning with God. All things came into being through him, and without him not one thing came into being. What has come into being in him was life, and the life was the light of all people. The light shines in the darkness, and the darkness did not overcome it" (John 1:1–5).

Jesus was God—eternal, Creator, Sustainer. Some of the disciples and friends of Jesus who stood watching His death from a distance had heard that affirmation from among themselves (see Matthew 16:13–16) and from the voice of God Himself (see Matthew 17:5) during their time with Jesus. They had seen His glory (see John 1:14) and they had seen His nobility, faithfulness and generosity under extreme suffering, even interacting with Him while He suffered on the cross (see John 19:25–27). Now—on that hill just over there—He was dead.

It was a humility that stooped into nothingness, into non-existence. Death always brings shattering and shuddering, but the death of God was so much more—world-shattering, universe-shuddering but also world-changing and world-redeeming.

Canadian novelist Douglas Coupland was once asked his greatest fear. He replied: "That God exists, but doesn't care very much for humans."[5]

In Jesus and His crucifixion, God conquered this fear: God does care, very much, for humans—"For God loved the world so much . . ." (John 3:16, NLT)—so much that He was prepared to sacrifice His existence to demonstrate that care, and to make possible our eternal reconnection, rescue and relationship with Him.

The stooping attitude

It is little wonder Paul uses these pictures of the humility and servanthood of a God who stoops as the greatest expression of God's glory and love—and how we are to live them out in our lives: "Let the same mind be in you that was in Christ Jesus, who, though he was in the form of God, did not regard equality with God as something to be exploited, but emptied himself, taking the form of a slave, being born in human likeness. And being found in human form, he humbled himself and became obedient to the point of death—even death on a cross" (Philippians 2:5–8).

In response to this goodness and overwhelming humility, we are to hold, practise and share our faith with that same humility. We expend ourselves—personally and corporately—in serving and seeking the best for those with whom we share our lives and our world. It is little wonder the prophet Micah linked the quest for justice and mercy with the imperative "to walk humbly with your God" (Micah 6:8).

The temptation of God's followers is to seek to reside with God on the mountaintops of spiritual experiences. This was Peter's ill-informed suggestion on the Mount of Transfiguration that they should set up shelters in that time and place (see Matthew 17:4). But this is not God's way. Practical humility is about coming down from the mountain to walk amid and with people who are lost, threatened or suffering, risking ourselves for their healing, helping and saving.

God still stoops

Jesus demonstrated His love by serving as "God with us" in a historical time and place in the messiness of our world. That is what He does in our lives in our various challenges and troubles. And that is what He is still doing in our world today, if only we look out for Him. God still

131

stoops to serve—you, me, us, everyone—even when we betray and deny Him. As both John and Paul described, it is Jesus' greatest act, showing the "full extent of His love."

After He had washed their feet, Jesus invited His disciples—as He also invites us—to join Him in this attitude and action: "So if I, your Lord and Teacher, have washed your feet, you also ought to wash one another's feet. For I have set you an example, that you also should do as I have done to you. Very truly, I tell you, servants are not greater than their master, nor are messengers greater than the one who sent them. If you know these things, you are blessed if you do them" (John 13:14–17).

While our ritual of splashing water on each other's clean feet at church is a way to imaginatively act out and engage with this story and a poignant reminder of Jesus' instruction, the greater call is to live—like Mary—both everyday and extraordinary lives of humility, service, love and gratitude for the One who loves us so much. And, as His disciples, we too stoop before the dirty feet of the people and the world He loves.

1. Margin note, New Living Translation.

2. See 1 Timothy 5:10, see also John Christopher Thomas, *Footwashing in John 13 and the Johannine Community*, Sheffield Academic Press, 1991.

3. Frederick Buechner, *The Magnificent Defeat,* New York: HarperCollins, 1985, page 105.

4. C S Lewis, *Miracles: A Preliminary Study* (1947), New York: HarperCollins, 2001, page 179.

5. "P.S. About the Author: Meet" in Douglas Coupland (1998), *Girlfriend in a Coma* (2004 edition), Harper Perennial, page 2.

Continuing on the Journey To Life

Reading and Responding to John's Gospel

Often we read Scripture out of a sense of duty or guilt. We somehow get the idea that we are expected to read, but we really do not understand what we are reading and we long to know more. In the past, has John's gospel been to you like Isaiah's gospel was to the Ethiopian eunuch? Philip asked the man, "Do you understand what you are reading?" And he replied, "How can I, unless someone guides me?" This book has been written to help guide readers to a better understanding of and appreciation for John's gospel. It is based on the conviction that we understand Scripture best when we invite others to "sit beside" us and we read together in community.[1]

John's gospel has long been treasured by Christian communities. Church members turn to it for its familiar verses, its images of Christ, and its stories of encounters with Jesus. When readers follow the theme of believing or "light" or "water" through its pages, they notice the artistry that carries John's rich theology.

This book has been written to help readers see the abundance that each new reader and reading brings, and the possibilities for responding to this story. We have followed the signs as they led us to new

135

understandings of Jesus. We have also wept with Jesus at gravesides, experienced the awe—and agony—of the enigmatic Jesus, questioned our own sectarian prejudice and the sanctioning of violence, and been challenged by a God who stoops down and washes the feet of the vulnerable and the voiceless.

The last part of this book invites your readings and responses. Since there will always be new readers in new situations bringing new questions to John's gospel, our journey is never done.[2] Instead, it continues, inviting ever-deepening understandings of Jesus, the focus of this gospel.

Included below are some questions for further reflection. Our hope is that they will spark many more questions, readings and responses to John's gospel. Under the guidance of the Spirit, we hope this book will give you richer views of Jesus and deepen your experience with "the Word made flesh." It is our prayer that your reading of John's gospel will lead you like signs on the journey to an ever-deepening encounter with the Jesus who promises abundant life.

Questions for Further Reflection

Introduction—Signs to Life: Reading and Responding to John's Gospel

1. Can you relate to the problem of the Ethiopian eunuch who was reading the words of Scripture but not really understanding them?
2. What do you see the seven "signs" (miracles) in John's gospel pointing to? If they are indeed signposts pointing in a particular direction, where does John hope his readers arrive?
3. What does it mean to listen to the readings of others? Is that a good thing? Can it be a dangerous thing?

PART I *SIGNS TO LIFE*: A READER'S RESPONSE

Chapter 1—Signs of Salvation

1. Is your mother the type of person who tries to "save the day" when something is amiss in a social situation?
2. Is this story about the type of beverage Jesus creates or about the quality of life Jesus offers? What assumptions do you bring to this first-century story?
3. Why do you think the author sets up this story by saying, "On the third day . . ." (John 2:1)?
4. What connections do you see between Jesus' first sign and the cross scene (John 19:23–37)?

Chapter 2—A Wedding at the Well

1. In one of her many works on John's gospel, scholar Gail O'Day says of the Samaritan woman that the "woman herself notes the scandal of their conversation."[3] What is scandalous about their conversation? How does this knowledge help you be a better reader of this story?
2. Are there any people whose plate or cup you would not share? What do you find offensive about them?
3. When did you first learn that Jesus was the "Christ"? Was your reaction anything like this woman's reaction? Why do you think this is the first time in John's gospel that Jesus identifies himself as the Christ?
4. Why does the narrator tell us that the woman "left her water jar" (John 4:28)?

Chapter 3—Belief Before Signs

1. Have you ever travelled a long distance in an attempt to get healing for yourself or a loved one? What did you think about along the journey?
2. Are you an "I'll-believe-it-when-I-see-it" kind of person? Is that a positive or negative quality? What might the author of John's gospel say to you?
3. How does the faith of others affect your own belief?

Chapter 4—The Sabbath as Sign

1. When you were a child, was your experience of the Sabbath primarily about rules or restoration? What about today?
2. What do you think becomes of the healed man after his encounters

with Jesus? Why do you think John's gospel leaves his story so open-ended?

3. In what ways does this particular sign anticipate Jesus' final conflict with the Jewish religious leadership?

Chapter 5—Signs of Liberation

1. What are your favourite religious festivals or holidays? Why do you particularly like them?
2. Have you ever been travelling and genuinely thought you might never see home again—due to severe air turbulence in a plane, an accident, an illness? What would it have meant to hear the words, "I am; do not be afraid"?
3. Does Jesus sound vulnerable when so many turn away from him (John 6:66) and he then asks the 12 disciples, "Do you also wish to go away?" (John 6:67)? Have you ever wondered about your own response to that question?

Chapter 6—Sign of God's Work

1. Have you ever had to choose between your faith and your family? If so, what does that experience bring to your understanding of the blind man's parents? Do you sympathise with them?
2. What is the most powerful part of the man's testimony? What is your testimony?
3. Why does John's gospel immediately go into Jesus' discourse about sheep and the Good Shepherd after Jesus "found" the blind man again (John 9:35–41)?

Chapter 7—Sign of Glory

1. Have you ever prayed words similar to Mary and Martha's letter to Jesus: "Lord, (s)he whom you love is sick" (John 11:3)?
2. Have you ever felt the mixture of despair, accusation and faith expressed in Martha's words: "Lord, if you had been here, my brother would not have died"?
3. What does it mean to you that "Jesus wept"?
4. What connections do you see between the raising of Lazarus and the raising of Jesus?

PART II *ABUNDANT LIFE*: READERS RESPOND

From Sorrow to Joy—Carolyn Rickett

1. What does the story of Lazarus mean when our loved ones are not brought back to us—when we experience "our own bereavement occasioned by an unhalted death"?
2. Have you ever experienced a sense of abandonment by God because of an experience of grief? What was the loss you experienced? Did you sense Jesus weeping with you?
3. What social rituals allow us to share in each other's grief? How do they help us in our experiences of loss?

The Enigma of Jesus in the Gospel of John—Daniel Reynaud

1. What is your reaction to Jesus as an enigma or mystery? Do you agree? What baffles you about John's Jesus?

2. Ironically, in John's gospel it is the blind man who "sees." Do you recall a time when you heard an amazing insight into Scripture or God from an unlikely source?

3. What is your reaction to the idea that prophecy is primarily a revelation about Jesus rather than prediction about the future? Do you agree or disagree?

The Samaritan "Other" in the Gospel of John—Jane Fernandez

1. How is the woman at the well "alien" to Jesus and to the first readers of John's gospel? In what ways is the woman "doubly marginalised"?

2. Who in your community is considered "alien" or "marginal"? Are there social situations in which you feel alienated or marginalised?

3. What is your reaction to the discussion of "sacred violence"? How do some forms of Christianity perpetuate the idea?

The God Who Stoops—Nathan Brown

1. Have you noticed all the "stooping" that goes on in John's gospel? Why do you think that is? What is the author saying about Jesus? What is the author hoping for his readers?

2. Jesus also stoops down in another scene, where a woman has been caught in adultery (John 7:53–8:11). Is the author linking her story to Jesus' act of stooping to earth and becoming one with humanity (John 1:1–14)? Is the author linking her story to Jesus' act of washing the feet of his disciples?

3. When in life do you find it easy to "stoop down" and serve? In which situations do you find such "stooping down" particularly difficult?

1. Stephen E Fowl and L Gregory Jones, *Reading in Communion: Scripture and Ethics in Christian Life*, Grand Rapids, MI: Eerdmans, 1991.

2. See Mikhail Bakhtin, *Problems of Dostoevsky's Poetics: Theory and History of Literature, No 8* (edited and translated by Caryl Emerson), Minneapolis, MN: University of Minnesota Press, 1984, page 166.

3. Gail R O'Day, "John's Gospel," in *Women's Bible Commentary* (3rd edition) (Twentieth-Anniversary Edition), (editors Carol A Newsom, Sharon H Ringe, Jacqueline E Lapsley), Louisville, KY: Westminster John Knox Press, 2012, page 521.

Suggested Resources

Additional conversation partners for reading and responding to John's Gospel

Introductions to John's gospel

Each of the following works contains a single, easily readable chapter devoted to introducing readers to the Gospel of John:

- Paul J Achtemeier, Joel B Green, Marianne Meye Thompson, *Introducing the New Testament: Its Literature and Theology,* Grand Rapids, MI: Eerdmans, 2001, pages 175–205. This resource represents an evangelical approach to studying the books of the New Testament written by a group of teachers.
- John C Brunt and Douglas R Clark (editors), *Introducing the Bible,* Vol 2, Lanham, MD: University Press of America, 1997, pages 235–47. Brunt and Clark are two Adventist writers who published this work while they were teaching in the theology department at Walla Walla College (now University).
- Mark Allan Powell, *Introducing the New Testament: A Historical, Literary, and Theological Survey*, Grand Rapids, MI: Baker Academic, 2009, pages 169–89. Powell has created additional online resources to accompany his introductory book. These may be found at <www. IntroducingNT.com>.

In addition to the above, R Alan Culpepper, *The Gospel and Letters of John*, Nashville, TN: Abingdon, 1998, is a helpful work providing more in-depth discussion of the various issues of authorship, time and place for the writing of John's gospel. One chapter of Culpepper's book considers the New Testament letters of John.

Literary and narrative studies of John's gospel

For readers interested in further exploring the literary techniques of John's gospel, the following works emphasise this approach:

- R Alan Culpepper, *Anatomy of the Fourth Gospel: A Study in Literary Design*, Philadelphia, PA: Fortress Press, 1983. This work was ground-breaking in 1983, as Culpepper illustrated the literary integrity of the gospel and introduced many Bible scholars to narrative criticism.
- Paul D Duke, *Irony in the Fourth Gospel*, Atlanta, GA: John Knox Press, 1985. Duke shows how irony works in John's gospel, and by doing so opens up possibilities for greater understanding.
- Susan E Hylen, *Imperfect Believers: Ambiguous Characters in the Gospel of John*, Louisville, KY: Westminster John Knox Press, 2009. Challenging previous theories that characters in this gospel are either "for" or "against" Jesus, Hylen shows the ambiguity of their descriptions, making them much more like contemporary believers in their imperfect following of Jesus.
- Robert Kysar, *John the Maverick Gospel* (3rd edition), Louisville, KY: Westminster John Knox Press, 2007. Taking a primarily literary approach, Kysar's third edition of this much-loved work shows how John's gospel is a theological "maverick."
- Francis J Moloney, "The Function of John 13–17 Within the Johannine Narrative," in *What is John?* Vol II (edited Fernando F Segovia), Society of Biblical Literature Symposium Series, Atlanta, GA: Scholars Press, 1998, pages 43–66. Moloney has long been appreciated for his scholarship on the gospel of John. In addition to numerous articles, he has also completed a three-volume commentary that is literary in its approach.

Studies in John's gospel noting particular reading perspectives

These works consider the perspectives brought to reading the Gospel of John by contemporary readers who are conscious of their particular locations:

- Colleen Conway, "Gender Matters in John" in *A Feminist Companion to John*, Vol II (editor Amy-Jill Levine), Cleveland, OH: The Pilgrim Press, 2003, pages 79–103. Conway not only notices the women in John's gospel, but she compares the way they are portrayed to the portrayal of key men within the narrative.
- Hisako Kinukawa, "On John 7:53–8:11: A Well-Cherished but Much-Clouded Story" in *Reading from this Place: Social Location and Biblical Interpretation in Global Perspective*, Vol. 2 (editors Fernando F Segovia and Mary Ann Tolbert), Minneapolis: Fortress, 1995, pages 82–96. In her reading of the story of the woman caught in adultery, Kinukawa notices the dishonour of the scene as similar to the stories of Asian women forced to be "comfort women" by the Japanese military during World War II.
- Craig H Koester, "The Spectrum of Johannine Readers" in *What is John?* Vol I (editor Fernando F Segovia), Society of Biblical Literature Symposium Series, Atlanta, GA: Scholars Press, 1996, pages 5–19. Koester shows how John's gospel was shaped for diverse readers, therefore a diversity of readers and readings should be welcomed today.
- Emerson B Powery, "African American Criticism" in *Hearing the New Testament: Strategies for Interpretation* (second edition) (editor Joel B Green), Grand Rapids, MI: Eerdmans, 2010, pages 326–49. In this short piece, Powery introduces and illustrates African–American criticism by modelling a reading of a scene in John's gospel.
- Adele Reinhartz, *Befriending the Beloved Disciple: A Jewish Reading of the Gospel of John*, New York: Continuum, 2001. As a Jewish Johannine scholar, Reinhartz brings a unique perspective to John's gospel.

Cultural and rhetorical studies of John's gospel

Readers interested in learning more about the cultural context of John's gospel will appreciate the following works:

- Bruce J Malina and Richard Rohrbaugh, *A Social-Science Commentary on the Gospel of John*, Minneapolis: Fortress, 1998. These scholars have been key voices in identifying the values of ancient Mediterranean culture throughout the New Testament. In this work, they focus on John's gospel.
- Jerome H Neyrey, *The Gospel of John in Cultural and Rhetorical Perspective*, Grand Rapids, MI: Eerdmans, 2009. Fortress Press calls Neyrey a "leader in the use of the social sciences in biblical studies." In this work, Neyrey reads John's gospel in the context of classical rhetoric and cultural anthropology.
- Beth M Sheppard, "Another Look: Johannine 'Subordinationist Christology' and the Roman Family" in *New Currents Through John: A Global Perspective* (editors Francisco Lozada, Jr and Tom Thatcher), Atlanta, GA: Society of Biblical Literature, 2006, pages 101–19. Sheppard argues for the importance of first-century Roman family life in order to understand the gospel's depiction of Christ's relationship to God.

Studies in John's gospel with particular attention to issues of power and identity

Readers interested in the intersection of contemporary questions of power with those of John's gospel will be challenged by the following works:

- Wes Howard-Brook, *Becoming Children of God: John's Gospel and Radical Discipleship*, Maryknoll, NY: Orbis Books, 1994. Writing from an American context, Howard-Brook takes a liberation theology interpretation of John's gospel and calls contemporary readers to respond politically and faithfully.

- Mary Huie-Jolly, "Maori 'Jews' and a Resistant Reading of John 5:10–47" in *John and Postcolonialism: Travel, Space and Power* (editors Musa W Dube and Jeffrey L Staley), London: Sheffield Academic Press, 2002, pages 94–110. Huie-Jolly, who has studied in Dunedin, New Zealand and currently teaches at the University of Winnipeg (Canada), explores why some Maori converts to Christianity began calling themselves "Jews" as a form of resistance against colonialism.
- Jean K Kim, "Adultery or Hybridity? Reading John 7:53–8:11 from a Postcolonial Context" in *John and Postcolonialism: Travel, Space and Power* (editors Musa W Dube and Jeffrey L Staley), London: Sheffield Academic Press, 2002, pages 111–28. Kim sees the setting for the woman caught in adultery scene as similar to that of colonised men who turn on the women of their own culture when such women are abused by their colonisers.

147

Select Bibliography

Adams, Richard Manly Jr, "Jesus did Many Other Signs: Aelius Aristides' Parchment Books and the Fourth Gospel's View of History," paper presentation, Society of Biblical Literature annual meeting, San Francisco, California, November 22, 2011,

Alter, Robert, *The Art of Biblical Narrative*, New York: Basic Books, 1981.

Anderson, Paul N, *The Riddles of the Fourth Gospel: An Introduction to John*, Minneapolis, MN: Fortress Press, 2011.

Ashton, John, *Understanding the Fourth Gospel*, Oxford: Clarendon Press, 1993,

Bakhtin, M M, "Art and Answerability," *Art and Answerability: Early Philosophical Essays* by M M Bakhtin (edited by Michael Holquist and Vadim Liapunov, translated by Vadim Liapunov), University of Texas Press Slavic Series, No 9, Austin, TX: University of Texas Press, 1990.

Bakhtin, M M, "Response to a Question from the *Novy Mir* Editorial Staff," *Speech Genres & Other Late Essays* (edited by Caryl Emerson and Michael Holquist, translated by Vern W McGee), Austin, TX: University of Texas Press, 1986.

Bigger, S, "Book Review: Ricoeur and the Hermeneutics of Suspicion," *Journal of Beliefs & Values: Studies in Religion & Education*, Routledge, May 2011.

Brown, Raymond E, *A Retreat with John the Evangelist: That You May Have Life*, Cincinnati, OH: St Anthony Messenger Press, 1998.

——, *The Gospel According to John I–XII*, The Anchor Bible series, Garden City, NY: Doubleday & Company Inc, 1966.

Burkert, W, René Girard, and Jonathan Z Smith, *Violent Origins: Ritual*

Killing and Cultural Formation, Stanford, CA: Stanford University Press, 1997.

Carter, Warren, *John: Storyteller, Interpreter, Evangelist*, Peabody MA: Hendrickson, 2006.

Clark-Soles, Jaime, "I will Raise [Whom?] Up on the Last Day: Anthropology as a Feature of Johannine Eschatology," *New Currents Through John: A Global Perspective* (edited by Francisco Lozada Jr and Tom Thatcher), Atlanta, GA: Society of Biblical Literature, 2006.

Culpepper, R Alan, *Anatomy of the Fourth Gospel: A Study in Literary Design*, Philadelphia, PA: Fortress Press, 1983.

———, *The Gospel and Letters of John*, Nashville, TN: Abingdon Press, 1998.

De Salvo, Louise, *Writing as a Way of Healing: How Telling Our Stories Transforms Our Lives*, New York: Harper Collins, 1999.

de Wit, Hans, Louis Jonker, Marleen Kool, Daniel Schipani (editors), *Through the Eyes of Another: Intercultural Reading of the Bible,* Amsterdam: Institute of Mennonite Studies, 2004.

Derrida, Jacques, *Learning to Live Finally: The Last Interview* (translated by Pascale-Anne Brault and Michael Naas), Hoboken, NJ: Melville House Publishing, 2007.

Duke, Paul D, *Irony in the Fourth Gospel*, Atlanta, GA: John Knox Press, 1985.

Esler, Philip F, and Ronald Piper, *Lazarus, Mary and Martha: Social-Scientific Approaches to the Gospel of John*, Minneapolis, MN: Fortress Press, 2006.

Frame, Janet, *The Lagoon and Other Stories: The Pocket Mirror*, New Zealand: Random House, 2004.

Girard, René, *Things Hidden Since the Foundation of the World,* Stanford, CA: Stanford University Press, 1987.

———, *Violence and the Sacred* (translated Patrick Gregory), Baltimore, MD: Johns Hopkins University Press, 1979.

Hylen, Susan E, *Imperfect Believers: Ambiguous Characters in the Gospel of John*, Louisville, KY: Westminster/John Knox Press, 2009.

Iser, Wolfgang, *The Act of Reading: A Theory of Aesthetic Response,* Baltimore, MD: Johns Hopkins University Press, 1978.

James, John W, and Russell Friedman, *The Grief Recovery Handbook,* New York: William Morrow, 2009.

Kelley, Melissa M, *Grief: Contemporary Theory and the Practice of Ministry*, MN: Fortress Press, 2010.

Kleinman, Arthur, *The Illness Narratives: Suffering, Healing and the Human Condition*, Basic Books, 1998.

Koester, Craig R, *The Word of Life: A Theology of John's Gospel,* Grand Rapids, MI: Williams B Eerdmans, 2008.

Kristeva, Julia, *Powers of Horror: An Essay on Abjection* (translated by Leon S Roudiez), New York: Columbia University Press, 1982.

Leader, Darian, *The New Black: Mourning, Melancholia and Depression*, London: Penguin Books, 2008.

Malina, Bruce, *The New Testament World: Insights from Cultural Anthropology* (revised edition), Louisville, KY: Westminster/John Knox Press, 1993.

Malina, Bruce, and Richard L Rohrbaugh, *Social-Science Commentary on the Gospel of John*, Minneapolis, MN: Fortress Press, 1998.

Martyn, James L, *History and Theology in the Fourth Gospel* (2nd edition), Nashville, TN: Abingdon, 1979.

———, *History and Theology in the Fourth Gospel* (3rd edition), Louisville, KY: Westminster John Knox Press, 2003.

Muddiman, John, and John Barton (editors), *The Gospels*, New York: Oxford University Press, 2010.

Müller, Ekkehardt, "The Jews and the Messianic Community in Johannine Literature," *DavarLogos*, vol 4 no 2, 2005.

O'Day, Gail R, *The Word Disclosed: Preaching the Gospel of John* (revised edition), St Louis, MO: Chalice Press, 2002.

_____, *Revelation in the Fourth Gospel: Narrative mode and theological claim*, Philadelphia PA: Fortress Press, 1986.

Painter, John, *The Quest for the Messiah: The History, Literature and Theology of the Johannine Community* (2nd edition), Nashville, TN: Abingdon, 1993.

Rando, Therese, *How to Go On Living When Someone You Loves Dies.* New York: Bantam Books, 1991.

Reinhartz, Adele, *Befriending the Beloved Disciple: A Jewish Reading of the Gospel of John*, New York: Continuum, 2001.

Segovia, Fernando F, "The Gospel of John," *A Postcolonial Commentary on the New Testament Writings* (edited by Fernando F Segovia and R S Sugirtharajah), T and T Clark, 2009.

Siker, J Yates, "Anti-Judaism in the Gospels According to Matthew, Mark, Luke, John, and Mel," *Pastoral Psychology,* vol 53 no 4 (March 2005).

Thomas, John Christopher, *Footwashing in John 13 and the Johannine Community*, Sheffield Academic Press, 1991.

Valentine, Gilbert M, *W W Prescott: Forgotten Giant of Adventism's Second Generation*, Hagerstown, MD: Review and Herald, 2005.

White, Ellen G, *Selected Messages* Book I, Washington, DC: Review and Herald, 1958.

Worden, J William, *Grief Counseling and Grief Therapy: A Handbook for the Mental Health Practitioner* (4th edition), New York: Springer Publishing Company, 2009.

Wright, H Norman, *The Complete Guide to Crisis & Trauma Counseling: What to Do and Say When It Matters Most*, California: Regal, 2011.

Wyckoff, Eric J, "Jesus in Samaria (John 4:4–42): A Model for Cross-Cultural Ministry," *Biblical Theology Bulletin: A Journal of Bible and Theology*, Sage, 2005.

Avondale

COLLEGE OF HIGHER EDUCATION

Avondale College of Higher Education provided a research grant to assist in the development of *Signs to Life: Reading and Responding to John's Gospel* and in the production of the accompanying CD. Avondale values excellence, spirituality and nurture. It accepts the challenge of learning and discovery, believes that nothing is of greater significance than each person's relationship to God as Creator, Redeemer and Sustainer, and seeks to encourage members of its learning community to realise their full potential, and to live full and joyful lives.

For more information about Avondale College of Higher Education, visit <www.avondale.edu.au>.